SO-BJR-424

THE EDUCATOR'S BRIEF GUIDE TO THE INTERNET AND THE WORLD WIDE WEB

Eugene F. Provenzo, Jr.

School of Education
University of Miami

EYE ON EDUCATION
6 DEPOT WAY WEST, SUITE 106
LARCHMONT, NY 10538
(914) 833–0551
(914) 833–0761 fax

Copyright © 1998 Eye On Education, Inc.
All Rights Reserved.

For information about permission to reproduce selections from this book, write: Eye On Education, Permissions Dept., Suite 106, 6 Depot Way West, Larchmont, NY 10538.

ISBN 1-883001-43-9

Library of Congress Cataloging-in-Publication Data

Provenzo, Eugene F.
    The educator's brief guide to the Internet and the World Wide Web / by Eugene F. Provenzo, Jr.
        p.   cm.
    Includes bibliographical references (p.) and index.
    ISBN 1-883001-43-9
        1. Internet (Computer network) in education. 2. World Wide Web (Information retrieval system) 3. Education—Computer network resources.   I. Title
    LB1044.87P76 1997
    025.06'37—dc21   97-25293
                                                                           CIP

10 9 8 7 6 5 4 3 2 1

Editorial and production services provided by Richard H. Adin Freelance Editorial Services, 9 Orchard Drive, Gardiner, NY 12525 (914-883-5884)

Published by Eye On Education:

Educational Technology: Best Practices from America's Schools
by William C. Bozeman and Donna J. Baumbach

The Educator's Brief Guide to Computers in the Schools
by Eugene F. Provenzo, Jr.

The Performance Assessment Handbook
Volume 1: Portfolios and Socratic Seminars
by Bil Johnson

The Performance Assessment Handbook
Volume 2: Performances and Exhibitions
by Bil Johnson

Block Scheduling: A Catalyst for Change in High Schools
by Robert Lynn Canady and Michael D. Rettig

Teaching in the Block
edited by Robert Lynn Canady and Michael D. Rettig

The Reflective Supervisor
by Ray Calabrese and Sally Zepeda

Handbook of Educational Terms and Applications
by Arthur K. Ellis and Jeffrey T. Fouts

Research on Educational Innovations
by Arthur K. Ellis and Jeffrey T. Fouts

Research on School Restructuring
by Arthur K. Ellis and Jeffrey T. Fouts

Hands-on Leadership Tools for Principals
by Ray Calabrese, Gary Short, and Sally Zepeda

The Principal as Steward
by Jack McCall

The Principal's Edge
by Jack McCall

Leadership: A Relevant and Practical Role for Principals
by Gary M. Crow, L. Joseph Matthews, and Lloyd E. McCleary

Organizational Oversight:
Planning and Scheduling for Effectiveness
by David A. Erlandson, Peggy L. Stark, and Sharon M. Ward

Motivating Others: Creating the Conditions
by David P. Thompson

Oral and Nonverbal Expression
by Ivan Muse

Instruction and the Learning Environment
by James W. Keefe and Harry M. Crenshaw

Interpersonal Sensitivity
by John R. Hoyle and Harry M. Crenshaw

Directory of Innovations in Elementary Schools
by Jane McCarthy and Suzanne Still

**The School Portfolio:
A Comprehensive Framework for School Improvement**
by Victoria L. Bernhardt

The Administrator's Guide to School-Community Relations
by George E. Pawlas

Innovations in Parent and Family Involvement
by William Rioux and Nancy Berla

Bringing the NCTM Standards to Life
by Lisa B. Owen and Charles E. Lamb

Mathematics the Write Way
by Marilyn S. Neil

School-to-Work
by Arnold H. Packer and Marion W. Pines

**Transforming Education Through Total Quality
Management: A Practitioner's Guide**
by Franklin P. Schargel

Quality and Education: Critical Linkages
by Betty L. McCormick

The Educator's Guide to Implementing Outcomes
by William J. Smith

Schools for All Learners: Beyond the Bell Curve
by Renfro C. Manning

ABOUT THE AUTHOR

Eugene F. Provenzo, Jr., Ph.D. is a Professor in the Social and Cultural Foundations of Education at the University of Miami. He is the author of a wide range of books on technology, education and history, including *Beyond the Gutenberg Galaxy: Microcomputers and the Emergence of Post-Typographic Culture* (New York: Teachers College Press, Columbia University, 1986), *Video Kids: Making Sense of Nintendo* (Cambridge, MA: Harvard University Press, 1991) with Arlene Brett, *Adaptive Technology for Special Human Needs* (Albany, New York: State University of New York Press, 1995), and *The Educator's Guide to the Computers in the Schools* (Eye on Education, 1996). He recently developed with Charles T. Mangrum II, an interactive hypermedia/electronic reading program for second and third graders entitled *Steck-Vaughn's World of Dinosaurs* (Austin, TX: Steck-Vaughn, Inc., 1993), as well as a thematically based middle school curriculum using the Internet *Learning OnLine* (N. Billerica, MA: Curriculum Associates, 1997). His research on computers and video games has been reviewed in the *New York Times*, *The Guardian*, and *The London Economist*. He has been interviewed on National Public Radio, Public Television, ABC News World News Tonight, the CBS Evening News, Good Morning America, The Leeza Gibbon's Show, BBC radio, Britain's Central Television and Britain's Channels 2 and 4, as well as Australia's LateLine.

For Charles T. Mangrum II
Colleague and friend and Internet explorer

For direct links to many of the sites described in this book, readers are invited to visit:

http://www.education.miami.edu/ep/iworkshop

TABLE OF CONTENTS

PREFACE

The Internet and the World Wide Web have the potential to be the most exciting developments in K-12, college, and university education in recent years. The Internet is important because it makes a series of extremely valuable tools and resources easily available to teachers and students.

First and foremost, the Internet provides students with the means by which to access huge amounts of information. There are literally billions of pages of data, graphic, sound, and motion picture resources available on the Internet. If you are interested in art, you can visit Web sites at the Louvre in Paris, the Metropolitan Museum of Art in New York City, or the National Gallery in London. The Library Congress, through its American Memory project, can provide the user access to thousands of photographs from the Civil War or the Depression, as well as documents on the American Constitution and African American history.

The Internet also provides teachers and students with tools such as e-mail that make it possible for them to talk to and exchange ideas, information, and experiences with virtually anyone in the world. Imagine students in an advanced high school French class in Los Angeles talking to their counterparts in an English class in Marseilles. Not only is it possible, it is being done regularly using the Internet and e-mail.

All that is needed to connect with the resources of the Internet are a basic computer and a telephone connection. As a teacher and educational researcher, I believe that the Internet and computers are setting in motion a revolution in education by "bringing the world to the child," or, conversely, by bringing the classroom to the world. Networked resources on a global level are now available to students at all levels of the educational system for minimal cost.

The pages that follow provide an introduction to the Internet and the World Wide Web for educators. My purpose is to provide a practical handbook for administrators and teachers, as well as to reflect on the potential of this new technology to redefine the traditional curriculum in elementary and high schools.

Besides being a resource in terms of technical issues and curriculum, this book is also a directory of Internet sites. I have collected hundreds of different web sites that I think are useful to educators. These Internet sites are highlighted To get to these sites, type the addresses in the address box of your Internet browser and hit enter. Visit my home page at the University of Miami—School of Education to be linked to a hyperlinked index that will take you directly to these sites by simply clicking on them.

I would like to thank Arlene Brett, Tom Dughi, Charles Mangrum, Gary McCloskey, and Alan Whitney for their help on this project. The Bellingham, Washington School District was generous in its permission to use materials from their program. Their assistance is greatly appreciated. Special thanks, as always, go to my wife Asterie Baker Provenzo.

I hope you find this book a useful guide to the Internet and the World Wide Web and that it helps you introduce new models of discovery and learning to the students in your classrooms and schools.

Eugene F. Provenzo, Jr.
Miami, Florida

1

INTRODUCTION

COMPUTER NETWORKS AND THE INTERNET

Computer networks are the basis of the Internet and the World Wide Web. Basically, a network connects one computer to another so that they can exchange information and communicate with each other.

What is a network?

A computer network connects one computer to another or many computers.

Networks can be small or very large. A network may be just one computer connected to and communicating with another computer. The computer that I am writing this book on, for example, is connected to a second computer on the other side of the room by means of a direct cable or null modem. Using a software package, I can send information between the two computers. This is a very simple network.

Any other computer network, including the Internet, essentially functions the same way. Two or more computers are connected together. In the case of the Internet, the only difference is the number of computers that can be connected and the protocols—the procedures and programs—that are used to keep them communicating with each other. It is estimated that there are 15 to 32 million computers currently linked worldwide through the Internet.

Many people think that all computer networks are part of the Internet. This is not the case. Many networks stand by themselves. The confusion lies in the fact that many freestanding computer networks can connect their users to the Internet. To the user it may appear that there is no difference between the smaller network system they are on and the Internet. You might think of a smaller network as being like a secondary road with its own shops and services. Access to a superhighway may be possible, but is not guaranteed.

In addition to the larger Internet structure, there are basically five different types of computer networks most users need to know about:

- ◆ **Commercial networks.** These are networks that anyone can subscribe to and include services like CompuServe, Prodigy, and America Online. These networks provide a wide-range of services including databases, electronic bulletin boards, and discussion groups. They charge a user fee or connect charge.

- ◆ **Nonprofit networks.** These are networks run by nonprofit organizations and that are generally dedicated to issues such as education, the environment, and peace. An example is Free-Net, a collection of local community networks intended to focus on the needs of local areas.

- ◆ **Private networks.** These networks are set up by a private business or public institution. An example is the network established by the Dade County Public Schools, which allows teachers and administrators to exchange information and to stay in contact with their colleagues throughout the district.

- ◆ **Regional Networks.** These are networks that serve a particular region. Big Sky Telegraph in Montana, for example, provides access to information exchange and communication in a particular area of the country where services are otherwise limited.

- ◆ **State Networks.** State networks are already operating or are proposed in virtually every state in the country. In Florida, for example, the FIRN system is a statewide educational networking system that provides educators a wide-range of information and communication services. (Freezer and Freezer, pp. 3–4)

What is a connect charge?

This is the fee that is paid to connect to a commercial communications service such as CompuServe or America Online.

Networks are an important new phase of the computer revolution. Just as there was a major shift in our understanding and use of computers as a result of the transition from mainframe to micro- or personal computing, a similar transition is now occurring as a result of the increasing use of networks such as the Internet.

The agricultural age was based on plows and the animals that pulled them; the industrial age, on engines and the fuels that fed them. The information age we are now creating will be based on computers and the networks that interconnect them.

Source: Michael L. Dertouzos, *Communications, Computers and Networks*

WHAT IS THE INTERNET?

The Internet is a network of computer networks. We can trace its beginnings back to the Soviet Union's launch of the satellite Sputnik in 1956. At that time the American military formed the Advanced Research Projects Agency (ARPA) to insure that the United States did not fall behind the Soviet Union in technology development. In 1962, theorists argued that it was possible to connect computers at different locations together in networks that allowed the computers to communicate with one another using a common language. Seven years later, in 1969, an experimental system known as ARPANET began operation. It connected computers at the University of California at Los Angles, Stanford Research Institute, and the University of Utah.

In 1972, the first electronic mail (e-mail) program was created. It allowed messages to be sent and received across the network. In 1984, the number of computers on ARPANET was more than 1,000. These computer sites were almost exclusively at research universities across the country. In 1986, the National Science Foundation (NSF) created the NSF Net backbone on ARPANET. Five supercomputing centers were set up to provide access to high-speed computing across the country.

What is the Internet?

The Internet is the successor to an experimental network built by the U.S. Department of Defense in the 1960s. Today, it is a loosely configured system that connects millions of computers around the world.

On the ARPANET, and its successor the Internet, no central computer controlled the network. Instead, many computers are connected to one another to exchange information. The result has been the creation of a huge network of computers linked together in a worldwide system. Using an Internet Protocol (IP) packet—which functions like a mailing envelope with an address on it—data can be sent between different computers on the system.

What is the ARPANET?

The ARPANET was a predecessor to the Internet funded by the Department of Defense.

Defining precisely what makes up the Internet is difficult. It's a moving target that continues to evolve. In the early 1990s, the Internet was made up of all of the computer networks connected together using the IP protocol. These networks were usually created by universities, government agencies, and regional and foreign systems. Recently, other computer networks that do not use the IP protocol have been connected to the Internet. Thus, a simple explanation of what the Net is becomes impossible.

The majority of computers in the world are not connected to the Internet. However, the gap between the number of computers in use throughout the world and the number of personal computers with Internet access is rapidly shrinking. The gap will continue to narrow in the final years of the decade. In 1996, there were approximately 234 million computers installed worldwide. Of these, 52 million had Internet access. Estimates for 1999 calculate that the worldwide installed base for personal computers will increase to approximately 303 million machines and that approximately 184 million of these machines will have Internet access. By 1999 the compound annual growth of personal computers with Internet access will be 68.4%, or four times the overall rate of installed personal computers. (Wilde, 1996, p. 21F)

If you think of the Internet as a worldwide information and computer network, it is easier to understand that it is also the first step toward the creation of the "Matrix" of Cyberspace—a vast information superhighway.

THE "MATRIX" AND CYBERSPACE

> **What is meant by "the Information Superhighway"?**
>
> The Information Superhighway refers to the idea of vast sources of information being avail-

William Gibson invented the term "cyberspace." It first appeared in his 1984 novel *Neuromancer*, where he describes a not-too-distant future when the world is dominated by powerful multinational corporations. Gibson's fictional world is tied together by an electronic construct called the "matrix." This is a vast electronic network that connects all of the world's computers and information systems. Its primitive origins are in video games and the Internet.

What is cyberspace?

According to science fiction writer William Gibson, cyberspace is: "A consensual hallucination experienced by billions of legitimate operators in every nation, by children being taught mathematical concepts.... A graphic representation of data abstracted from the banks of every computer in the human system. Unthinkable complexity. Lines of light ranged in the nonspace of the mind, clusters and constellations of data. Like city lights, receding...." Cyberspace has come to mean the place where data is transferred back and forth in our worldwide computer systems.

To navigate the massive electronic database of the matrix, users are connected, or interfaced, through electrodes wired to their brains. The graphic representation the user sees in order to navigate through the matrix—the simulation itself—is called cyberspace.

Michael Benedikt, a professor of architecture and design at the University of Texas describes cyberspace as:

> A new universe, a parallel universe created and sustained by the world's computers and communication lines. A world in which the global traffic of knowledge, secrets, measurements, indicators, entertainments, and alter-human agency takes on form: sights, sounds, presences never seen on the surface of the earth blossoming in a vast electronic night. (Benedikt, p. 1)

Cyberspace has become a reality in the form of the Internet and the World Wide Web. It is a place where students and teachers, and the culture in general, will spend greater and greater amounts of time. We are experiencing a time similar to the beginning of the Renaissance, only a few years after Johannes Gutenberg invented moveable type. Just as it took many decades to discover the possibilities of the new book culture, so, too, are we just beginning to discover the possibilities of the Internet, the World Wide Web, cyberspace, and beyond.

WHY USE A NETWORK?

There many different things that you can do on a computer network. A few examples are:

♦ **Electronic Mail.** Electronic mail (e-mail) is one of the most common uses of networks. Basically, e-mail allows you to send messages on an almost instantaneous basis from one computer to another.

♦ **Bulletin Boards.** Bulletin Boards (BBS) provide a place for the public discussion of issues. A topic is identified and then people electronically post notes on that topic which may be of interest to others.

What is the World Wide Web (WWW)?

The World Wide Web is a browsing system that makes it possible to navigate the Internet by pointing and clicking one's computer mouse. The Web connects diverse sites by the use of hyperlinks.

♦ **Conferences.** A common feature on many computer networks is conferencing which allows "real time" exchanges between individuals.

♦ **Databases.** A huge number of databases on different subjects are available on almost all of the larger networks.

What is a Web site?

A Web site is a collection of documents found on a single computer server or set of servers.

♦ **Listservs.** Listservs are electronic messages or information that are distributed to lists of individuals interested in a specific topic.

♦ **File Transfer Protocol (FTP).** This a set of procedures that allow you to send data to another computer on a network. (Frazier and Frazier, pp. 5-6)

What is hypertext?

Hypertext is a model for presenting information in which text becomes linked in ways that allow readers to browse and discover the connections between different sets of information.

What is hypermedia?

Hypermedia is any combination of text, sound, and motion pictures included in an interactive format on the computer. Hypermedia is an extension of hypertext emphasizing audio and visual elements.

What is Hypertext Markup Language (HTML)?

Hypertext markup language is a coding system for creating hypertext links on Web documents.

What is a hyperlink or link?

A hyperlink or link is a highlighted graphic such as a button or illustration, or piece of text that connects a user to another web site or source of information or file on the Internet.

What is a Web browser?

A Web browser is graphical user interface that is used to view documents on the Web.

What is ftp (file transfer protocol)?

A file transfer protocol allows a user to be transferred across different sites on the Internet.

What is telnet?

Telnet allows access to computers and their databases, typically at government agencies and educational institutions.

What is a gopher?

A gopher is a menu-based system for searching data on the Internet.

What is WAIS?

WAIS (Wide Area Information Server) is a computer server that allows full-text keyword searches of information resident at sites on the Internet.

What is a home page?

A home page is a web screen that acts as a starting point to go to multiple sites on worldwide computing networks.

BASIC ELEMENTS OF A WEB PAGE VIEWED THROUGH A BROWSER

URL Link: This box shows the address or home page you will go to if you click on

Title: This is the title for the Web site

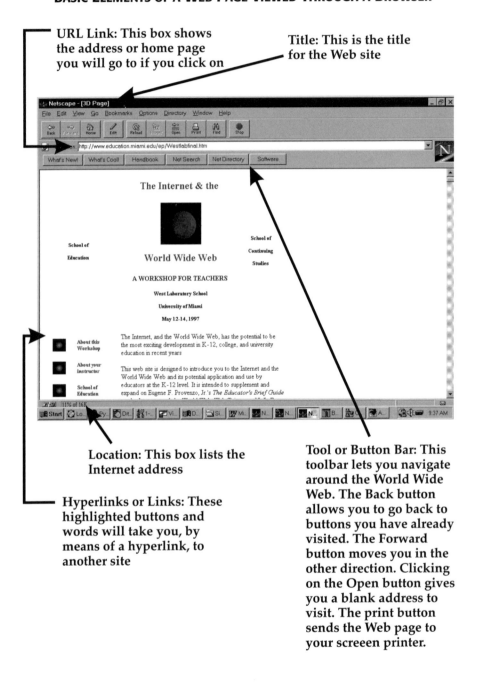

Location: This box lists the Internet address

Hyperlinks or Links: These highlighted buttons and words will take you, by means of a hyperlink, to another site

Tool or Button Bar: This toolbar lets you navigate around the World Wide Web. The Back button allows you to go back to buttons you have already visited. The Forward button moves you in the other direction. Clicking on the Open button gives you a blank address to visit. The print button sends the Web page to your screeen printer.

SOME COMPUTER NETWORKS OF INTEREST TO EDUCATORS

There are many different types of commercial computer networks available to educators including:

America Online
8610 Westwood Center Drive
Vienna, VA 22182
800-827-6364

Classroom Prodigy/Prodigy
445 Hamilton Avenue
White Plains, NY 10601
800-776-3449

CompuServe
PO Box 20212
Columbus, OH 43220
800-848-8990

GEnie
401 N. Washington St.
Rockville, MD 20850
800-638-9636

GTE Educational Network Services
1090 Vermont Avenue NW, Suite 800
Washington, DC 20005
800-659-3000

National Geographic Kids Network
5455 Corporate Drive, Suite 104
Troy, MI 48007
800-246-2986

Scholastic Network
555 Broadway
New York, NY 10012
800-246-2986

Nonprofit networks of interest to educators:

NASA SpaceLink
George C. Marshall Space Flight Center
Mail Code CA21
Huntsville, AL 35812
by modem: (205) 895-0028
spacelink.msfc.nasa.gov
192.149.89.61

National Public Telecomputing Network (Free-Nets)
PO Box 1987
Cleveland, OH 44106
(216) 247-5800
fax (216) 247-3328
info@nptn.org

PBS Online
1320 Braddock Place
Alexandria, VA 22314
(703) 739-5000

Like Florida's FIRN (Florida Information Resource Network), many states have set up educational networks to provide low cost access to list serves and bulletin boards, as well as access to the Internet. Look into this possibility in your own state as a means of being able to get on line easily and cheaply.

THE WORLD WIDE WEB

The World Wide Web (WWW) is one of the most exciting areas of contemporary computing. Instead of being a computer network, the Web is a network of information that is resident on the Internet. First proposed in 1989 by the European Particle Physics Laboratory (CERN) in Switzerland, the Web was designed as an information-sharing system for physicists throughout the world.

The Web is important in that it creates a continuous network of information in a consistent format. In doing so, it overcomes the problems of incompatibility between different computer systems and networks.

One of the most interesting features of the Web is Hypertext Markup Language (HTML). This is a special means of coding documents on the Web which allows hyperlinks or links to other parts of the same document or other sites on the Internet.

The Web has become enormously popular because of its speed and easy accessibility. In addition, it presents graphic information and video and sound files which make going online an engaging multimedia experience. The Web is also very easy to navigate. Up until the introduction of the Web, going online was too difficult for most people. Various protocols and command strings had to be inputted into machines. The process was often tedious and confusing.

The Web is highly visual and intuitive. Almost anybody can use it with just a couple of minutes of instruction. Using a Web browser, older Internet tools such as ftp (file transfer protocol), telnet, e-mail, gopher and WAIS, can be easily accessed and used. Using your computer mouse, you can simply point and click and navigate through the Internet.

On page 12 is an illustration of the home page for a Web site developed by this book's author and displayed with the Netscape Web browser. Browsers like this and Microsoft Internet Explorer are the main tools for exploring the World Wide Web. Think of the browser as the control panel that allows you to navigate around a web page or to go to another site.

THE INTERNET AND THE WORLD WIDE WEB AS A FORCE FOR EDUCATIONAL CHANGE

The Internet and the World Wide Web have the potential to redefine traditional schooling. By providing a worldwide information resource, connectivity to students and teachers on a global basis, relatively low cost, and ease of use, the Internet and the World Wide Web open resources that were only dreamed about a few years ago.

The Internet and the World Wide Web also change our models of instruction. Teachers are not so much dispensers of information using the Internet and the World Wide Web, but guides in the discovery of new knowledge. Teaching and learning have the potential to be transformed by this new technology in ways that will ultimately be of major benefit to our children and culture.

The pages that follow are intended to provide a basic guide to those interested in using this new and exciting technology in their schools. I hope to answer most of your questions and to describe the possibilities for using the Internet and the World Wide in your classrooms and schools.

2

GETTING CONNECTED TO THE INTERNET

CONNECTING TO A NETWORK

Connecting to a network such as the Internet is a relatively straightforward task. You need a computer, a modem, and a telephone line. You can use a regular telephone line, but be aware that while a computer is connected to it, the line cannot be used for regular calls.

Connection to a network is made with a modem. A modem is an electronic device that allows you to connect your computer to a telephone and to send messages via a telephone line. Modems convert digital signals from the computer (0s and 1s) to audio signals which are sent just as your words are when you speak into a voice piece.

What is a modem?

A modem is an electronic communications device that allows a computer to send and receive data over a standard telephone line. The modem itself is run by means of a communications program that is resident on the computer where the modem is installed.

Modem speeds are measured in bits per second (bps). This is what is called a baud rate. A couple of years ago, standard modem speeds were 2400 bps. Now they run anywhere from 14.4 to 28.8Kbps (kilobytes per second), and are getting faster all of the time.

Modem speed is important because it determines how fast information can be received. As more use is made of large and data-intensive graphic and sound-based programs on networks such as the Internet, the speed at which information can be transferred becomes even more important. Always get the fastest and most reasonably priced modem possible. This not only saves you time, but it also reduces connect and online service costs. You can buy a 56Kbps modem for as little as $150.

What is baud rate?

Baud rate refers to the speed at which a modem can transmit data. The baud rate of modems has increased significantly in recent years. The faster the baud rate of a modem, the quicker it can transfer information over a telephone line. Faster modems are more expensive but save telephone connect time and are necessary for efficient use of the Internet.

Along with a modem, you also need a software program or communications package to run it. These are almost always provided with the modem. You may find it helpful, however, to use a different communications package than the one that comes with the modem. This decision is best discussed with a staff member or consultant who is knowledgeable in the field.

Commercial networks charge a series of fees for use of their services. These are often provided at a deep discount to educators and schools. You will need to find out how to establish a network account with your provider.

Access to any network is done with a password. This prevents other people from accessing your account. A password is like the key to your house. Other people should not have it except under special circumstances. Choose a password that is easy for you to remember. The title of a favorite book, a friend, or a geographical place are just a few suggestions for good passwords. Remember, a password, like a secret, only works if it is kept confidential and not shared with other people.

What is a password?

A password is a code word that lets you access a computer account. It protects against unauthorized use of an account.

HOW POWERFUL A MACHINE DO I NEED TO GET ACCESS TO THE INTERNET?

MACINTOSH REQUIREMENTS

You do not need the most powerful machine to get onto the Internet. Any Macintosh computer with at least four megabytes of RAM, a hard drive of at least 80 megabytes and a 14.4 or 28.8Kbps modem will work very well. You will also need a modem program, which is usually provided by your Internet service or your commercial online service.

IBM/WINDOWS REQUIREMENTS

As is true of the Macintosh computer, you do not need an extremely powerful machine to get Internet access. A 386 or 486 processor will work, as will a Pentium processor. Four megabytes of RAM and a hard drive of at least 80 megabytes is needed. A 14.4 or 28.8Kbps modem and a modem program are also needed.

HOW UP-TO-DATE DO MY COMPUTER AND MODEM NEED TO BE TO GET ACCESS TO THE INTERNET?

One of the dilemmas continually facing educators using computers is whether their equipment is current enough. The answer is one that you have to determine for yourself. Does your equipment and software do what you need to have it do for you? In the case of the Internet and the World Wide Web, does it get you to the sites you are interested in visiting? Can you download the material you want without excessively long waits? Do you have adequate storage on your hard drive?

Computer equipment is in a constant process of evolution. The most current computer equipment that you can buy will be outdated within a few months. Gordon Moore, one of the pioneers in computer chip manufacture, argued in the mid-1960s that the number of transistors that could be put on an integrated circuit would double every two years. This means that computer power would also double at the same rate. This principle became known as Moore's Law. The law has been modified and now states that the number doubles every 18 months and increases fourfold every 3 years. Because basic prices for computers tend to remain constant, this means that the computer you bought 18 months ago can be bought for the same price today, but with twice the computational power.

What is Moore's Law?

Moore's Law was first formulated in 1964 by Gordon Moore, one of the cofounders of the computer chip manufacturer that became Intel Corporation. He argued that the number of transistors that could be put on an integrated circuit would double every two years. The law has been modified and now states that the number doubles every 18 months and increases fourfold every 3 years.

Using anything less than a 386 machine or a modem that is slower than 14.4Kbps is not practical. Be careful not to buy outdated equipment at fire sale prices. Older equipment is generally cheaper because it is outdated.

HOW DO I GET CONNECTED TO THE INTERNET?

There are two ways to get connected to the Internet. One is through a **commercial online service** such as *CompuServe*, *America OnLine*, or *Prodigy*. These services provide specialized chat lines and bulletin boards, as well as access to various specialized data files such as newspapers and magazines. Commercial online services tend to provide a set amount of free time per month and then charge on an hourly basis. This is rapidly changing, however, as prices and provided services are becoming more and more competitive between Internet providers. Access to the Internet is relatively easy through most online services.

The second way to get access to the Internet is through an **Internet service provider**. An Internet service provider offers direct access to the Internet and the World Wide Web. Its services are much more limited than most commercial online services. It is also usually cheaper to use.

Before choosing an Internet service provider (ISP) make sure that the service you are using is dependable. There are usually a wide-range of available ISPs in most communities. Try to learn from other users whether the service you are considering is dependable. Does it provide telephone support for technical issues? Is the support free?

How much will it cost per month for the service? Does the service include unlimited access or a limited number of hours after which you are charged a per-hour charge for connect time? How fast is the system? Can you purchase space on the system to post your own Home Pages?

You can look for ISPs in your telephone book's Yellow Pages. In addition, if you have Internet access (perhaps through a friend or local library), you can do a search of Internet service providers. A good address to starts at is:

Internet Service Providers
   http://www.currents.net/resources/netprov/
   netprov.html

NAVIGATING THE INTERNET AND THE WORLD WIDE WEB

There is a clear logic to Web site addresses. The key is the idea of a Uniform Resource Locator or URL. A URL has two parts. Look at the following address:

http://thomas.loc.gov/

This is the address for the United States' Congressional Web site. The **http://** indicates a World Wide Web address. The **thomas.loc.gov** part of the address is the specific address for the online site where the program is located. The **.gov** designation tells you that this is a government organization sponsoring the Web site. If it had a **.edu** designation, it would mean that the site was sponsored by an educational group. Think of a URL as being similar to a street address, which gets more specific as you get closer to the name.

What is a Uniform Resource Locator or URL?

A Uniform Resource Locator (URL) is like an address for a Web site. It tells your computer where the Web site is and who is in charge of it.

Until recently, the Internet was very difficult to use effectively for research. The Internet was too much like a giant, used bookstore where there are all sorts of interesting materials to be found but no effective shelf-list or catalogue to help locate them.

It was also difficult to take full advantage of the Internet because its search tools were fairly complicated and awkward to use. This changed with the World Wide Web's introduction of new types of search engines and directories.

Some of the most useful search engines are:

Lycos
http://www.lycos.com
Info Seek Guide
http://www2.infoseek.com
Excite
http://www.excite.com
Alta Vista
http://www.altavista.digital.com
Web Crawler
http://home.netscape.com/escapes/search/
netsearch_9.html

Search engines send out software "agents" or "spiders" that search every available web site and create huge indexes of materials.

Similar to search engines are data bases which provide extensive listings of Web sites in a directory format. Some of the major directories are:

> **Yahoo**
>   http://www.yahoo.com
> **Magellan**
>   http://www.mckinley.com

The difference in the type of information you get by using a search engine or a directory is not clear to most users. Generally speaking, directories are better for browsing for information and search engines are better for finding information on a narrow topic. Thus, if you were interested in finding Web sites that deal with the Smithsonian Institution in Washington, DC, you will want to use a directory such as Yahoo. If you are interested in finding all of the references to a particular type of dog such as a beagle, you might want a more site specific search. Using a search engine would not only bring sites devoted to beagles, but also information related to beagles, such as animal nutrition Web sites, Web sites on American dogs, and so on.

With the introduction of the World Wide Web, text-based search engines such as Gopher have become obsolete. Particularly for educators at the K-12 or beginning college level, where ease and accessible is critical, Web search engines and directories are the way to go.

CAN MY SCHOOL AFFORD TO GO ON THE INTERNET AND THE WORLD WIDE WEB?

Many people assume that they cannot use the Internet in their classroom because of limited funds. Almost any school can afford Internet access. A new computer in the $1,000 price range will connect you to the Internet. An older machine (at least a 386 processor) can be bought second-hand for even less, or possibly obtained as a contribution from an interested business or parent. Access to the Internet requires a telephone line and a service provider who typically charges between $15 and $30 per month. Such costs can be covered through supplemental funds or through special fundraising efforts by children and parents.

> For schools that already have computers and access to a single telephone line, the costs for daily collaboration with a class on the other side of the world can be modest; students in the inner city can be in contact with their peers in the global village for as little as a one time cost of less than $50 for a modem to connect the computer to a phone line. The cost for connection to the Internet, the full-fledged information superhighway, almost nothing ranges from minimal or none, if routed through universities to other facilitating institutions, to the more substantial fees being charged on the open market (amounting to several hundred dollars per year).
>
> Source: Cummins and Sayers, *Brave New Schools*

A computer with a modem can be set up in a centralized lab or media facility, or can be placed on a portable cart and moved around from classroom to classroom. Determine what is best for you based on how many telephones are available in your school. If you have trouble getting a dedicated telephone line, find out if there is a telephone anywhere in your school that is not being used during the day. Perhaps there is a special office—a night school program or volunteer agency—where the phone is used only occasionally. You may be surprised by what is available.

3

THE INTERNET AND EDUCATION

THE INTERNET AND THE WORLD WIDE WEB AS REDEFINING THE CURRICULUM

The Internet and the World Wide Web have the potential to redefine many aspects of the curriculum by bringing extraordinary information and communication resources into the schools. Students are able to reach beyond the confines of their classrooms and local communities to gather information and meet people from around the world.

Yet this extraordinary new tool creates a great deal of confusion. Teachers and schools are struggling with how to go beyond just using the Internet as an interesting place to browse—a fun place to "mess around"—and to use it instead as a curricular resource.

How can the Internet and World Wide Web best be used to help students learn? Can this new technology be integrated into traditional curriculums? If so, how?

Here are a few of the things we know that the Internet and the World Wide Web can provide to students in the classroom:

- ♦ Access to information from data sources and archives around the world;
- ♦ Access to libraries, magazines, and journals;
- ♦ Access to students on a national and global basis to have as pen pals, or with whom to collaborate and do joint research projects;
- ♦ Access to scientists and scholars;
- ♦ Access to graphic and sound files to use in creating various types of projects.

For teachers, the Internet and the World Wide Web can provide all of the above, as well as:

- ♦ Access to teacher lesson plans;
- ♦ Access to advanced training and instruction;
- ♦ Access to other teachers and people interested in classrooms.

Kathy Rutkowski, a teacher who has a Web site at

http://www.chaos.com/learn/KNOWLEDGE.html

argues that, "the Internet is a global intelligence community and as such it offers all learners ACCESS to information in a raw and unprocessed form as well as an enhanced form from around the globe, the means to PROCESS and EVALUATE the information, and, finally, the means to DISSEMINATE and PUBLISH the acquired knowledge." According to Rutkowski, the Internet should not be thought of not so much as a teaching tool but as a teaching space.

I think that Rutkowski summarizes a lot of what is most exciting, from an educational point of view, about the Internet and the World Wide Web. As a model of learning it fits how most people actually use information in the real world, information that is meaningful and important to them. Jim Cummins and Dennis Sayers believe that the Internet opens a new social and cultural dimension to learning. According to them:

> Teachers and students participating in the learning networks we have observed are clearly not engaged in trivial pen-pal activities, rather, they are conducting significant intercultural learning projects, such as joint surveys on drug abuse, homelessness, and teenage pregnancy in two communities, sharing and analyzing their results, and eventually publishing their findings in their local school or hometown newspapers. By opening their classrooms and their minds to experiences from other cultures, they are not unwittingly turning their backs on their own. In fact, these students have become more aware of their own culture as a result of the contrast they have experienced with another. (Cummins and Sayers, 1995, p. 13)

TECHNOLOGY AND ITS USE IN THE SCHOOLS: AN HISTORICAL PERSPECTIVE

Larry Cuban (1986) notes that instructional technology has been largely resisted by teachers and the educational system in general. Teachers often resent having new technologies imposed on them without their being consulted.

Why has instructional technology so often failed? Here are three possible answers:

1. Teachers often lack the training and skills necessary to make effective use of instructional technology.

2. Equipment and media are often expensive.

3. Equipment is not always reliable or dependable—often it is not available when needed. Instructional materials may not adequately fit students' instructional needs.

Source: Larry Cuban *Teachers and Machines*, p. 18; discussion of why films have not been more widely used in the schools.

What looks like a useful educational innovation by district leaders, local university consultants, or an enthusiastic principal, may rightly be viewed as an unwanted intrusion by a teacher.

Administrators and teachers need to clearly understand how computers can be effectively used in existing curriculums and school environments, and how they can bring about meaningful innovation and improvement. The essential question is: "How can computers and technologies like the Internet and the World Wide Web actually help teachers in their day-to-day work?"

Looking at earlier models of instructional technology can provide us with suggestions as to the types of things that will contribute to the effective implementation of computers in classroom instruction. Chalkboards, for example, came into widespread use in classrooms during the early nineteenth century because they allowed teachers much more flexibility and choice in their day-to-day work. With a chalkboard a teacher can "write, draw, erase, and keep materials for days; diagrams, quizzes, assignments, and insights that spontaneously erupt in discussions—all can be scrawled on the board." (Cuban, p. 58)

How can the Internet and World Wide Web be integrated into your teaching? How can they help you achieve your goals as an instructor?

To answer these questions you must think carefully about what it is you are trying to teach. The Internet and the World Wide Web are not very good for drill and practice. The very nature of the Internet directs students towards exploration and making judgments on their own.

This does not mean that traditional curriculum content cannot be incorporated into Internet activities. Students can learn basics, while being Internet explorers. They can develop skills while collecting new information and evaluating the usefulness of certain resources. In doing so, students can learn and enhance basic skills, as well as learn to be critical thinkers and independent researchers.

There are many ways these goals can be achieved. Professor Charles T. Mangrum II and I developed a series of books for Curriculum Associates, Incorporated called *Learning OnLine* that specifically lead students through traditional curriculum requirements. Designed as 16-page, thematically oriented explorations of high interest topics on the World Wide Web, the series is targeted at students at the middle school level. Each book in the series focuses on a specific topic. The first three books are *Apollo 11*, *The Wright Brothers and the Invention of Powered Flight*, and *Endangered Animals*.

Learning Online (Curriculum Associates)
http://www.ultranet.com/~cainfo/

After introducing each student to the thematic topic of the book, a series of online explorations are undertaken in mathematics, social studies, and language arts. Using the Internet and resources found on the World Wide Web, students address high interest thematic units, as well as practical problems using information drawn from online inquiries. In mathematics, for example, students go to a Web site at the Curriculum Associates offices in Massachusetts and connect into a *Learning On-Line* home page. There, they are able to connect directly to Web sites appropriate to the topic they are exploring.

Welcome to the Learning OnLine home page!

Learning OnLine is a program that will help you learn how to conduct research on the Internet's World Wide Web.

Not sure what the Web is? Click on a highlighted word to read its definition -- or just go straight to the Learning OnLine Glossary.

Using this Web site and your **Learning OnLine** books, you and your classmates can explore the far reaches of the Internet to find information about exciting topics such as space travel, the invention of powered flight, and endangered animals. As you do your research, you can use your browser to mark favorite Web sites with bookmarks.

Ready to get started? Click the hyperlink for the topic you want to explore. This will take you to the home page for that topic.

 Apollo 11

 Endangered Animals

● *The Wright Brothers*

The "Connection to Science" page in the *Apollo 11* book, for example, includes these questions:

- If you were to visit the site of the first moon landing today, what would you find?
- Why is there no life on the moon?
- What color is the moon?
- What are the two main types of terrain on the moon?
- What covers most of the surface of the moon? What is this material called?
- How old were most of the rocks found on the surface of the moon? What can these rocks tell us that Earth's rocks cannot?
- Before scientists had moon rocks to study, what were the three most common explanations for the origin of the moon?
- What is the current theory about the origin of the moon?
- Michael Collins described the moon as "a moving target." What did he mean by this? How would this fact complicate the job of scientists who planned *Apollo 11's* flight?

Each of these questions is of high interest, takes place in the real world, and requires integrating science skills and knowledge with electronic information gathering.

This example suggests how the Internet and the World Wide Web can be used to meet traditional curricular goals. Its innovative possibilities are just beginning to be explored. For example, what happens to the traditional field trip when put into an online context?

ELECTRONIC FIELD TRIPS

Electronic field trips can be taken by students almost anywhere in the world using the Internet and the World Wide Web. Through the Passport to Knowledge program, for example, middle school students join different teams of scientists around the world to conduct experiments.

Projects included as part of Passport to Knowledge have been *Live from the Stratosphere* (no longer available online), *Live from Antarctica*, and *Live from the Hubble Space Telescope*. In *Live from Antarctica*, researchers working in Antarctica corresponded with students via e-mail. In addition, students had electronic access to field journals being kept by researchers, as well as relevant databases and encyclopedias. Sponsored by Public Television, NASA, and the National Science Foundation, the Passport to Knowledge series also includes interactive television broadcasts and a wide-range of student and teacher materials.

Live From Antarctica
    http://www.gii-awards.com/nicampgn/232e.htm
Live from the Hubble Space Telescope
    http://quest.arc.nasa.gov/interactive/hst.html/

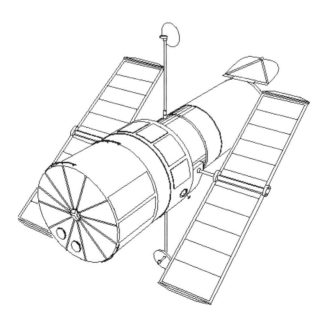

**Line drawing of the Hubble space telescope from
"Live from the Hubble Space Telescope" Web site**

Other programs also make it possible for students to go on electronic field trips. *Project Jason* (Project Jason Foundation for Education) is a live interactive distance learning project that has students and teachers join Dr. Robert Ballard (Senior Scientist at Woods Hole Oceanographic Institution) to investigate water habitats in southern Florida including the Florida Keys and the Everglades.

Project Jason
  http://www.jasonproject.org

Museums of every type can be visited using the World Wide Web. While many of these sites are limited to descriptions of exhibits and collections, others actually allow the visitor to look at specific collections, as well as to visit different virtual galleries. Some museum sites you might want to consider visiting as part of an online field trip include:

The Franklin Science Institute Museum
  http://sln.fi.edu/tfi/welcome.html
The Field Museum
  http://www.fmnh.org
The Virtual Museum of Computing
  http://www.comlab.ox.ac.uk/archive/other/
  museums/computing.html
Sistine Chapel
  http://www. science.wayne.edu/~mcogan/
  humanities/sistine/ceiling/index.html
The Smithsonian National Air and Space Museum
  http://ceps.nasm.edu:2020/NASMpage.html
The United States Holocaust Memorial Museum
  http://www.ushm.org
University of California Museum of Paleontology
  http://ucmp1.berkeley.edu
The Louvre
  http://mistral.culture.fr/louvre/

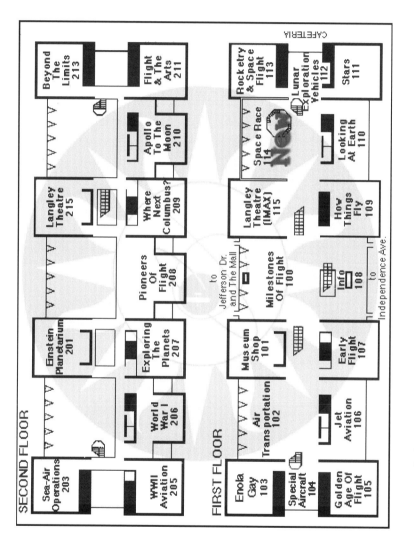

By clicking on the map included on the home page of the National Air and Space Museum, you can visit the different galleries in the Museum.

COLLABORATIVE PROJECTS OVER THE INTERNET

One of the most interesting opportunities provided for students using the Internet is to conduct joint projects with one another. The Global Attraction Project, for example, which ran February to June 1996, brought students in grades 4 to 12 from around the world together to compare gravitational attraction at different locations of the globe. The project had students calculate acceleration due to gravity in their individual locations and then e-mail their reports to the project's Web site.

Global Attraction Project
http://woody/lopernet.net/projects/gareg.txt

Cooperative projects can bring students together from across the country and globe in shared learning experiences. In doing so, students are required to go beyond their own experience, to share with others, and to consider alternative points of view. A recent project connecting Russian and U.S. citizens is Friends and Partners.

Friends and Partners
http://solar.rtd.utk.edu/friends/home.html

ELECTRONIC BOOKS

Imagine having at your fingertips all of the great books of the world. This is possible through the Internet. One of the most interesting uses of the Internet has been the creation of massive collections of online or electronic books. Most of these works have been put online by university-based scholars who are interested in establishing definitive electronic editions that they can use in conjunction with their research. Look for the many different sites available as part of Project Gutenberg to get a sense of the types of resources that are available.

Project Gutenberg
http://www.promo.net/pg/

If you are interested in reference books, they are available from many different sites on the Internet. Works such as the *CIA World Factbook,* the *Bible,* and the *Koran,* as well as the American Declaration of Independence and the Constitution can be found on the Internet through the World Wide Web. Encyclopedias such as *Britannica Online* are also available, although after an initial visit, access to the site requires payment.

Britannica Online
   http://www.eb.com/
CIA Factbook
   http://ftp.netnet.net/pub/aminet/docs/etext/
   world94.readme
The Bible
   http://www.mit.edu:8001/people/aaronc/
   bibles.html
The Koran
   http://etext.virginia.edu/koran.html

References sources you may want to take a look at include:

Grolier's Encyclopedia
   http://gagme.wwa.com/~boba/grolier.html
Roget's Thesaurus
   http://www.thesaurus.com/?
Virtual Reference Desk
   http://thorplus.lib.purdue.edu/reference/
   index.html
Webster's Dictionary
   http://c.gp.cs.cmu.edu:5103/prog/webster
World Atlas on the Web
   http://pubweb.parc.xerox.com/map/

DOES THE INTERNET HAVE TO BE IN MY CLASSROOM TO USE IT IN THE CURRICULUM?

Many schools may not be able to afford an Internet workstation in every classroom, but most can at least have one in the library. For the price of a basic Macintosh or Windows-based computer plus a modem, a service provider, and a telephone line, a school can be connected to the Internet.

When you set up such a computer you open the vast resources of the Internet to your students. Make sure that you post an Acceptable Use Policy for the machines. Once word gets out about how the Internet can be used, you will have to set up a schedule for students to go online.

If your school cannot fund an Internet site, or is reluctant to do so because of safety and security issues with students, then consider connecting from home. There are few more valuable and convenient resources for teachers interested in developing creative lesson plans and curriculums for their classes. Besides general sources of information, whether it is the Smithsonian, the National Air and Space Administration, or the Library of Congress, or some place else, teachers can draw on the efforts of other practitioners in the field.

4

INTEGRATING THE INTERNET INTO THE CURRICULUM

There are hundreds of ways that the Internet and the World Wide Web can be integrated into standard classroom curriculums. By its very nature, the Internet pushes instruction toward interdisciplinary models. Multiple sources of information can be consulted, different perspectives addressed. Sorting out all of the possible uses of the Internet becomes a real challenge.

The following activities are meant to provide models of how the Internet can be used with existing curriculums. Many cross different grade levels and subject areas. For example, an online tour of the Sistine Chapel can be used at the elementary level as part of an art lesson, or for a World history class at the secondary level.

The challenge for educators at all levels is to go beyond simply using the Internet for fun and to integrate it into the curriculum as a powerful instructional tool. New lesson strategies need to be planned, curriculums revised, and innovative instructional units developed, which take full advantage of the Internet's unique capacity to deliver instruction.

This is an evolutionary process that will take a significant amount of time. It is a process that will also be confusing at times as false starts are made and as Internet technology becomes faster and more sophisticated.

Read through the following activities. Think about how they might apply to your own classroom settings and how you could modify them for your own purposes. If you are a secondary English teacher, for example, think about how different Internet resources will suit your specific instructional needs. If you are reading a Civil War novel such as Stephen Crane's *Red Badge of Courage,* have students view photographs from the

Civil War or read diaries of soldiers who fought in the war to enhance your curriculum. What tools are available online which might help your students create written reports?

Model curriculums are presented in Chapter 5. You can use the sources and ideas in this chapter and in the rest of the book to develop your own curriculums to make full use of the power of the Internet and the World Wide Web.

Talk to colleagues about how they think the Internet and the World Wide Web can be used. Visit different web sites online to learn about what other teachers are doing. Find examples of curriculums already online that you can adapt for your class.

Here are just a few suggestions you might want to pursue on your own. The boxed material preceding each description includes subject areas where these activities might be used in the curriculum.

CREATE A SCAVENGER HUNT

Social Studies	Science	Humanities	Language Arts

Choose a topic such as the *Apollo 11* mission or the artwork of Picasso. Research sites to find things your students can use— for example, a photograph of a footprint on the moon, a painting from Picasso's Blue Period. Then let them loose to use search engines and their own skill to find the items. Students can work in teams or alone. They can also create scavenger hunts for other students.

This type of activity can be used in almost any subject and at any grade level. High school Biology students can conduct a scavenger hunt for parts of the body, collecting illustrations and specific information on anatomical functions. Fourth graders interested in the moon can find information on its geology or on the first manned lunar landings. A freshman English student could find information about a specific author or work of literature.

RESEARCH A CONTEMPORARY PROBLEM

Social Studies   Science   Language Arts

Have students research a current issue such as endangered animals or global warming. Students can present written reports or oral reports on their findings. They can create bulletin board reports, write action letters to politicians and public officials, and organize for action in their own communities.

This type of activity can be used at almost all grade levels. The Internet and the World Wide Web not only become a huge electronic information resource, but a place for students to talk to others, exchange information, and publish and share materials.

GET A PEN PAL

Social Studies   Humanities   Language Arts

Have students go online to find a pen pal from another part of the country or from abroad. Students can practice writing skills, a foreign language, create bulletin board displays, and present oral reports.

This activity can be used in larger curriculum units on global understanding, as well as in foreign language courses and writing and composition activities. It is particularly well-suited to students at the middle and secondary school levels.

Global Schoolhouse Project (provides pen pal exchanges)
http://gsh.cnidr.org/gsh/gshwelcome.html

RESEARCH A FAVORITE TOPIC

Social Studies   Humanities   Language Arts

Have students research a topic that they are interested in such as sports, stamp collecting, horseback riding, the Olympics, flying, or surfing. Have them design a bulletin board display, or prepare a class presentation or a written report on the subject.

Think of how these various topics can be integrated into the regular curriculum. How can a student's interest in stamp collecting be used to develop a greater understanding of geography? Can an interest in flying be linked to developing mathematical skills (computing the distance capability of different airliners with different fuel loads), or an interest in surfing lead to an examination of the scientific principles underlying wave motion?

VISIT A TOWN OR COUNTRY

Social Studies	Humanities	Language Arts

Have students visit a town or country on the Internet. Have them collect as much information as possible and present it in the form of a written or oral report. Students can create bulletin board displays. This type of project can be easily integrated into a foreign language program.

This activity can be used at almost any grade level, and can provide the basis for much greater geographical and cultural understanding. It can also help students in developing presentation skills as a result of presenting written and oral reports.

TRACK A STOCK

Social Studies	Mathematics	Language Arts

Have students select a stock and track it historically or on a day-by-day basis. Research the company whose stock is being tracked Asks students to graph their stock and its financial history, as well as present reports on the companies they are tracking.

This activity can provide students with exceptional opportunities to learn about doing research, compiling information and analyzing it. It can be linked to the real world by having students choose stocks and then discover if their choices are good ones.

Stock Market Data from MIT
    http://www.ai.mit.edu/stocks

This site provides recent stock market information, including previous day's closing prices, as well as historical statistics on the market.

NEWSPAPER OR NEWSLETTER EXCHANGE

Social Studies	Humanities	Language Arts

Establish an exchange of school or classroom newspapers and newsletters with another school. These can be sent via the Internet as attached e-mail items.

This activity can be integrated into almost any grade level. Students can practice writing and art and design skills while actually producing documents that will be read and shared by others.

CONDUCT A SURVEY

Social Studies	Mathematics	Language Arts

Have students develop a survey on a topic that interests them that they can distribute to other schools sites and e-mail addresses across the country. Compile the results from the surveys and have the students send back their reports to the people from whom they received their data.

Students at all levels can learn about constructing questionnaires, collecting data and analyzing it. Topics can be of interest and relate to needs of a local community, or be of particular interest to students (What are your favorite activities? What is your favorite movie? What do you think is the most important problem facing Americans?).

VISIT THE *NEW YORK TIMES*

Social Studies	Language Arts

Have students visit the *New York Times* or some other newspaper online. Ask them to look for articles about their state and/or community. Or have them compare the *New York Times* coverage of a specific event or issue with coverage provided by their local newspaper. Let them use models from the newspaper to write news pieces about their own community.

A source like the *New York Times* provides an excellent opportunity to introduce students to current events. Newspaper sites can also be used as the basis for writing activities dealing with current events, editorials, personalities and so on.

The New York Times
   http://www.nytimes.com

VISIT THE UNITED NATIONS

Social Studies   Language Arts

Have students go to the United Nations to collect information for reports and presentations on the organization and its history. Have students develop debates topics in which they represent different countries based on research they conduct online.

Researching the United Nations can be linked to world history courses, as well discussions about international affairs.

Electronic field trip to the United Nations
   http://www.pbs.org/tal/un/

RESEARCH A CAREER

Social Studies   Science   Humanities
Mathematics   Language Arts

Let students go online to research possible interests they have in different types of careers. Students can present written and oral reports on their findings, develop a career profile, or write a strategy for achieving their career goals.

Career education programs are common in middle school and high school curriculums. Have students explore different career opportunities. Another activity is to have students profile a specific profession and the goals that must be achieved to enter it. Career Mosaic provides an extensive database on jobs, including information on salaries, career opportunities and geographic location.

Career Mosaic
  http://www.careermosaic.com:80

Career Web is an extensive Internet site dealing with careers.

Career Web
  http://www.cweb.com

CREATE A VIRTUAL CITY

Social Studies   Science   Humanities
Mathematics   Language Arts

Have students visit and contribute to the construction of a three-dimensional virtual city by having them visit CitySpace. Students can create a bulletin board exhibit on an ideal city, or develop a report on their own town or city dealing with its problems and needs.

This type of activity can be used in conjunction with civics classes, as well as with lessons in ecology.

CitySpace
  http://www.cityspace.org

EXPLORE A FOREIGN LANGUAGE

Social Studies   Humanities   Language Arts

Have students visit a major foreign language site such as Le Coin Des Francophones at autres Grenouiiles, a site for those interested in French. Let them explore foreign language documents and resources, and talk to others in the language that interests them.

Sites such as this are ideal for foreign language instruction. Students can connect to others who are interested in sharing their language and culture. Vocabulary can be learned, as well as customs from other countries.

> **Le Coin Des Francophones at autres Grenouilles**
> http://laureline.freenix.fr/~elrond/aiguillage/
> themes/details/grenouilles.html

EXPLORE AFRICAN-AMERICAN HISTORY

Social Studies   Humanities   Language Arts

As part of Black history week or the more general social studies and humanities curriculum, students can explore different facets of African-American history. Have them choose a specific historical figure such as W.E.B. DuBois or Harriet Tubman to write a report or create a poster about this person.

Sources on African-American history can be linked to traditional curriculum units in American history courses, as well as to literature courses where Black authors may be relevant. The African-American Mosaic is a great source of information put together by the Library of Congress on every aspect of African-American history.

> **The African-American Mosaic**
> http://www.vmedia.com/alternate/restricted/
> wwww/data/sec3/subsec3/list11.htm

RUSSIA AT THE TIME OF THE CZARS

Social Studies   Humanities   Language Arts

The Internet has a number of outstanding sources on Russian history and culture. Have students explore these sites and discuss why the czarist government was brought down by the Revolution. Students can compile reports on the causes of the Revolution, as well as on key historical figures such as Czar

Nicholas II or Lenin. Research materials can be presented as oral reports or in other formats.

Activities of this type can be linked to Russian language courses at the secondary level, as well as courses in European or World history. To learn about the history of Russia before the Communist Revolution visit:

Alexander Palace Time Machine
http://www.travelogix.com/emp/batchison/

THE AMERICAN CIVIL WAR

Social Studies	Humanities	Language Arts

What were the causes of the American Civil War? Where did it occur? Whom did it affect? Have students explore the history of the war, as well as national battlefield sites such as Bull Run and Harper's Ferry. Reports, bulletin boards, and posters about the war can be created to share with others.

This activity can be connected to American history courses, as well as curriculums dealing with state and local history. For an extensive archive of Civil War materials see the Civil War Photographic Collection. This is a project sponsored by the Library of Congress that contains more than 1,000 photographs from the Civil War. It is an invaluable resource for students interested in the period.

Civil War Photographic Collection
http://rs6.loc.gov/cwphome.html

DISCOVER AMERICAN HISTORY THROUGH PHOTOGRAPHS

Social Studies	Humanities	Language Arts

The Internet is an incredible resource for historical photographs. The very best collection of American documentary photographs can be found at the American Memory Project sponsored by the Library of Congress. Have students visit this site to develop illustrated reports on the Civil War, the history of their state or local community, as well as topics such as women's history.

The American Memory Project is one of the most sophisticated historical sites available anywhere on the World Wide Web. It contains extensive photographic and archival collections that should be of interest to students at almost any level.

The American Memory Project
http://rs6.loc.gov/amhome.html

Using historical photographs can be a great supplement to Social Studies classes from elementary through high school. Harness the energy of upper level students to put together linked web sites and collections of photographs.

ART OF OTHER CULTURES

Social Studies	Humanities	Language Arts

Have students seek out information about art in other cultures. Encourage them to look at topics on a comparative basis; for example, the depiction of children or animals across different cultures and historical periods. Have them complete written reports or make a list of interesting Web site addresses on art in other cultures that they can share with classmates and other students.

This type of activity fits in well with curriculum units in social studies and multiculturalism. For an excellent database of Asian art exhibitions, research articles, and related types of materials visit:

Asian Arts
http://www.webart.com/asianart/index.html

QUOTABLE QUOTES

Humanities Language Arts

Discuss a topic that is of interest to students such as love, war, or the weather, and have them search through *Bartlett's Familiar Quotations,* the most famous American quote book, for a quote about the subject. Have them copy the quote. Conduct a class discussion in which students share their quotes and discuss them with one another.

This type of activity can be used from elementary through the secondary school level. Students can use a quote as a starter for an essay, create a poster using its words, create an anthology of quotes on a subject, or begin a collection of quotes they like for other reasons.

Bartlett's Familiar Quotations
http://www.cc.columbia.edu/acis/bartleby/
bartlett

GLOBAL SHOW N TELL

Social Studies Science Humanities Language Arts

The Internet makes it possible for students to share their artwork and writing on an international basis. Help students link up to a Show N Tell site on the Internet to learn how to submit their own work for posting on the Internet.

Show and tell is an excellent activity for elementary and middle school students. It can be integrated into a whole range of activities ranging from the preparation of reports on special topics to the creation of stories, poetry and artwork. The Global Show N Tell site lets children visit and present their own "Show and Tell" projects on a global basis.

> **Global Show N Tell**
> **http://www.manymedia.com/show-n-tell/**

RESEARCH A FOREIGN COUNTRY

Social Studies   Language Arts

Have students choose a foreign country that they are interested in. Have them find a map of their selected country, identify its main exports and the important moments in its history.

This activity can be integrated into Social Studies curriculums at almost all levels. Mapping skills can be emphasized, as well as global understanding and history.

For a historical tour of the British Isles, including England, Ireland, and Wales, visit:

> **History of the British Isles**
> **http://www.georgetown.edu/labyrinth/**
> **subjects/british_isles/british_isles.html**

For links to sites dealing with Latin American visit:

> **Latin American Studies**
> **http://lanic.utexas.edu/las.html**

RESEARCH HORSES

Social Studies	Science	Language Arts

Horses are a subject of enormous interest to many children. Have students discover all kinds of facts about horses as well as the history of the horse by going online. (Other animals, such as lions, elephants, and reindeer, can also be similarly researched.)

The study of horses or any similar animal can be the starting point for many different curriculums. How did horses change warfare in Western history? What was their effect on agriculture? What role have other animals such as dogs and cats, or cows and sheep, played in our lives?

Everything you need to know about horses and the role they have played in human culture and history can be found at:

The International Museum of the Horse
http://www.imh.org

DISCOVER OTHER STUDENT WRITERS

Social Studies	Humanities	Language Arts

Have students go online to discover writing by other young people. This type of activity can help students get started on their own writing. By seeing the writings of students such as themselves, they can begin to work on developing their own voice as writers.

KidLit is a site whose main purpose is to involve kids with literature. It includes reviews by students, student writings, and related types of materials.

KidLit
http://mgfx.com/kidlit

REDISCOVER LEONARDO DA VINCI

| Social Studies   Science   Humanities   Language Arts |

Leonardo da Vinci is one of the greatest thinkers, inventors, and artists of all times. There are many online sources for students to explore his life and art.

This activity provides an excellent opportunity for biographical exploration and the study of science, invention, and art. It can be part of a high school European history or Humanities class, or an art class at almost any level.

For pictures by Leonardo da Vinci visit:

Leonardo da Vinci Pictures
http://sop.geo.umn.edu/~reudi/leonardo.html

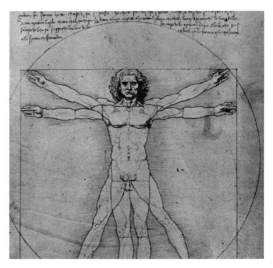

**Pictures created by Leonardo da Vinci, such as this "Palledian Man,"
are easy to find on the Internet and World Wide Web.**

VISIT THE WORLD'S GREAT MUSEUMS

Social Studies	Science	Humanities	Language Arts

Museums are a natural place for innovative web sites. Have students choose a museum (art, natural history, history, and so on) that is of particular interest to them. Have them visit it online and report back to their classmates about highlights and subjects of particular interest.

Excellent connections through this type of activity can be made to almost any subject in the curriculum. Visits to Natural History museums can supplement a science unit on dinosaurs, while a trip to the Louvre can be part of a European history course or an advanced course in French. The Louvre is one of the world's greatest art museums online. Its site includes information on the museum as well as on its exhibits, and detailed information on the major works and artists included in the Louvre's collections.

The Louvre
    http://mistral.culture.fr/louvre/

CALCULATE INTEREST

Social Studies	Mathematics	Language Arts

Various sites on the Internet make it possible to calculate mortgage interest. Have students calculate the difference between a mortgage on a house at different percentage points. Have students construct word problems for one another that require the use of a mortgage calculator.

Use this type of activity to supplement a math class on calculating interest. It can also be used in teaching home economics, business, and related subjects.

The Mortgage Calculator site provides a calculator where students can calculate the cost of a mortgage according to different repayment schedules. It is a good place for basic lessons in economics.

Mortgage Calculator
http://ibc.wustl.edu/mort.html

EXPLORE MATHEMATICS

Mathematics

Many Internet sites have extensive activities for students in Mathematics.

The Math Forum is a valuable site for students and teachers providing information on mathematics, as well as classroom activities. Sites like the Math Forum are ideal for bringing fresh ideas into the Mathematics curriculum at all levels of instruction.

Math Forum
http://www.forum.swarthmore.edu

CREATE A TIMELINE OF AVIATION HISTORY

Social Studies	Science	Mathematics	Language Arts

Have students create timelines on the history of aviation beginning with early ballooning experiments and continuing to the present. A classroom timeline can be created on a bulletin board with photographs and other illustrations as an additional project.

An activity like this can be linked to Social Studies classes. Students can create histories of specific airplanes, as well as biographies of famous aviators. NASA is one of the best sites for space- and science-related materials on the Internet.

National Aeronautics & Space Administration
http://hypatia.gsfc.nasa.gov/NASA_homepage.html

ADOPT A PLANET

Science   Mathematics

Have students adopt a planet and learn as much as they can about it from the Internet. Students can compile a book with illustrations to be shared with others.

Excellent possibilities for Basic Science classes, as well as courses in Physics. NASA provides rich visual sources and text on the planets.

Nine Planets Tour
   http://edgechaos.com/DEST/space.html

LOOK FOR THE BEST IN BOOKS

Social Studies   Humanities   Language Arts

Have students visit online bibliographical sources to develop lists of books that are of interest to them.

This is an ideal site for any class in literature. Materials from this type of activity could also be of use in History and Social Studies classes. Online Children's Books is an excellent source for children's literature.

Online Children's Books
http://www.iatech.com/books/intro.html

EXPLORE THE RAIN FOREST

Social Studies	Science	Language Arts

Have students set off on an assignment to discover why many of the world's rain forests are threatened. Ask them to develop a list of things that can be done to save the rain forests.

Learning about the rain forests of the world can be integrated in geography lessons, as well as Biology, Ecology, and Social Studies classes. The Rain Forest Action Network connects to environmental activists interested in saving the rain forests.

Rain Forest Action Network
http://www.ran.org/ran

EXPLORE THE ATOMIC BOMB

Social Studies	Science	Humanities	Language Arts

Nuclear weapons threaten our future. Students can explore the consequences of these weapons of destruction and the horror of nuclear war by visiting a number of sites. Have students create a poster showing the consequences of nuclear war and why we must avoid using nuclear weapons.

An excellent starting place for a curriculum dealing with the Cold War. Literature courses can link to poetry of the Atomic era. Photographic studies can also use this type of activity.

For a photographic tour commemorating the bombing of Nagasaki at the end of World War II visit:

> Remembering Nagasaki
> http://www.exploratorium.edu/nagasaki/

RAISE THE TITANIC

Social Studies	Science	Mathematics	Language Arts

The Titanic has fascinated people since it sank in 1912. Have students study the Titanic to capture a glimpse of what the world was like in the years just prior to World War I.

This is an ideal starting point for a unit on European and American history prior to World War I, as well as for units on life styles the history of transportation. Everything you want to learn about the Titanic can be found at:

> **Titanic Home Page**
> **http://gil.ipswichcity.qld.gov.au/~dalgarry/**
> **main.html**

ADOPT A DINOSAUR

Social Studies	Science	Language Arts

Kids and adults are fascinated by dinosaurs. Have students research a favorite dinosaur and put together a profile of it to share with other class members. Combine these profiles to create a dinosaur encyclopedia.

Dinosaurs are a great source for classes in Ecology, as well as Natural Science. They are particularly exciting for elementary and middle school students, but are also of interest to older students who can create dinosaur databases and discuss the causes of their extinction. For an interactive natural history museum where students learn about the fossil record, visit:

> **University of California Online Museum of Paleontology**
> **http://ucmp1.berkeley.edu**

DETERMINE POPULATIONS

Science   Mathematics

Have students visit the United States Census Bureau to collect information about the current population of the country, their state, and their local city or town.

This activity can be used in civic classes, current events, and Social Studies classes in general. Extensive census databases are available through this next site:

United States Census Bureau
http://www.census.gov

VIRTUAL DISSECTION

Science

For practice, before actually doing a dissection of a frog or other animal, have students visit a simulated dissection kit or program and have them conduct a dissection in cyberspace such as the one listed below where a frog can be dissected online.

This is an excellent activity for students in science and particularly biology courses.

Virtual Frog Dissection Kit
http://george.lbl.gov/ITG.hm.pg.docs/dissect/
info.html

ONLINE RESEARCH

Social Studies   Science   Humanities
Mathematics   Language Arts

Have students visit one of the numerous sites that have access to online reference sources. Create a list of things they must find: definitions for words, synonyms, location of strange and distant places, and so on.

This activity can be used across almost any subject in the curriculum where students need access to reference information.

The Research-It site provides an online dictionary, a thesaurus, a quotation finder, maps, foreign language dictionaries, financial data, and other useful research tools. The site is a must when a good library can't be gotten to easily.

Research-It
http://webcrawler.com/select/refbook.56.html

EXPLORE THE HOLOCAUST

Social Studies   Humanities   Language Arts

The Holocaust is one of the most tragic events of the twentieth century. Have students study the Holocaust by going to online sites where they can learn more about it. Students can develop oral and written reports. Use this opportunity to talk to students about the nature of persecution and intolerance.

This activity can be integrated into courses in European and American history, as well as literature courses. Studying the Holocaust is an obvious starting point for discussing the nature of prejudice and the need to tolerate differences in peoples and cultures. The Holocaust Memorial Museum site will help you plan a trip to the Museum, as well as do research and participate in educational activities.

The United States Holocaust Memorial Museum
http://www.ushmm.org

DISCOVER THE WHITE HOUSE

Social Studies   Humanities   Language Arts

Have students explore the White House and its history. Ask them to write the script for a tour through its hallways, which they would give if they were tour guides at the First Family's Home. Have students write the President via e-mail about an issue or topic that is of interest to them.

This activity can be used in American history classes, as well as special theme classes focusing around events such as a presidential inauguration.

For general information about the White House and the First Family visit:

White House
    http://www.whitehouse.gov

To meet Socks the cat and other important individuals connected to the White House, visit:

The White House for Kids
    http://www2.whitehouse.gov/WH/kids/html/
    home.html

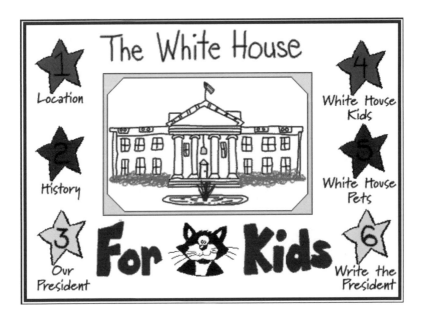

STUDY AN ANIMAL IN YOUR REGION
OF THE COUNTRY

Social Studies	Science	Humanities	Language Arts

Have students research an animal that is associated with their region of the country and have them learn more about it through different sites on the Internet. Have them develop reports on the animals of their choice.

An activity such as this can be easily integrated into sciences classes, as well as courses on local history and culture. In the case of literature, students can discover whether certain animals mentioned in the stories they are reading are associated with their part of the country, or even with the part of the country the story is about. How do the animals fit into a region's local economy, folk traditions, and ecology?

The Wolf Studies Project site, for example provides teachers and students in Minnesota with a clearinghouse for the exchange of information about wolves and their behavior, as well as access to migration data on wolves who have been electronically tagged in the Superior National Forest.

Wolf Studies Project
http://www.wolf.org

VISIT YOUR COMMUNITY

Social Studies	Science	Humanities
Mathematics	Language Arts	

Various map systems available on the Internet make it possible to zoom in on a specific spot or community. Have students visit your community to discover if they can actually find a map of your school's location or their neighborhood. A variation of this activity is to take a copy of a newspaper and ask students to locate maps of the different places that are mentioned in its articles.

This is an excellent activity for helping students develop mapping skills. It can be used in different ways at almost any grade level.

The site below was developed by the same people who invented the computer mouse, computer icons, and hypertext! It has a map of the world and gives you the opportunity to zoom in on an area that is of interest. You can print your own maps whenever you like.

Xerox Parc Map Viewer
   http://pubweb.parc.xerox.com/map/

EXPLORE POETRY

Social Studies	Humanities	Language Arts

Many universities are setting up literature archives online. At the University of Virginia there is an extensive archive of British poetry. Have students focus on a single British poet's life and work. Among just a few of the poets whose work is represented are Lewis Carroll, Samuel Taylor Coleridge, Ann Batten Cristall, Alfred Edward Housman, Richard Polwhele, Mary Robinson, Dante Gabriel Rossetti, and Alfred, Lord Tennyson.

British poets are just a starting point. Consider exploring American poets for history and social studies units you are teaching. What about biographies of famous poets, or poems about famous things or places (Walt Whitman and the Brooklyn Bridge, for example)?

British Poetry (1780–1910)
   http://etext.lib.virginia.edu/britpo.html

Additional literature sources are provided at:

Bartleby Library, Columbia University
   http://www.columbia.edu/acis/bartleby/
   index.html

THE POETRY CORNER

Humanities   Language Arts

Having students write their own poems and sharing them with others is a wonderful experience. The Internet provides many places for students to submit their poems for online publication. Poems students write can be shared in class and published on a classroom web page or as part of a school anthology.

This is a great activity for almost any class where students are creating poetry or doing writing of their own. Links to modern and contemporary poetry are found at:

Links to Modern and Contemporary Poetry
http://lang.nagoya-u.ac.jp/~nagahata/
Poetry.html

MYTHOLOGY

Humanities   Language Arts

Have students explore ancient mythology. Possible projects include creating an encyclopedia of myths, comparing myths across cultures, or exploring myth archetypes. An interesting project for students is to have them research the origins of the names of the days of the week and the months of the years.

This activity can be integrated in literature courses as well as European history. An excellent source for Greek and Roman myths is:

Myths and Legends
http://thecocean.uoregon.edu/myth/~myth/

EXPLORE LANGUAGES

Social Studies	Humanities	Language Arts

Most students have no knowledge of the extraordinary number of languages found throughout the world. Have students visit online sources dealing with different languages. Have them compare different words across cultures. For example, what is the word for woman or man in Chinese, Spanish, Latin, Italian, Romanian, German, and French? Is there any possible connection between the words?

This type of activity is a natural for use in foreign language courses at any level. Also, secondary courses that have units on linguistics might find this type of activity useful.

This next site is a massive index with links to hundreds of sources about language from around the world.

The Human-Languages Page
http://www.june29.com/HLP/

VISIT ANOTHER CITY

Social Studies	Mathematics	Language Arts

It is easy to visit different cities using the Internet. Most municipal governments and chambers of commerce have created Web sites that include maps, demographic information, historical material, and photographs. Have students explore a city that interests them to develop reports, or have them do research on where they live.

This is a great activity for teaching students about geography. It can also be used in English Composition or Social Studies classes with students writing essays on cities, creating maps, or compiling graphs of demographic information (The Sites to See in New York City!) and so on. For online tours of major American cities visit:

Citylink Project
    http://www.neosoft.com:80/citylink/

WORLD GEOGRAPHY

Social Studies   Language Arts

The Internet is an extraordinary place to explore geography. Have students go to sites around the world to collect information about faraway places and cultures. Students can create travel brochures, write reports about different cultures and places, as well as create posters and bulletin boards. Oral reports let them discuss what they have learned with other classmates.

This is a great activity for almost any type of Social Studies class.

City Net is an outstanding guide to different communities and countries from around the world:

City Net
    http://www.city.net

An excellent guide to different communities around the world is:

Einet Galaxy Index to World Communities
    http://galaxy.einet.net/galaxy/Community/
    World-Communities.html

THE CENSUS

Social Studies   Mathematics   Language Arts

There are few data sources as rich as the United States Census. Have students visit the U.S. Census Bureau site to find data about different parts of the country, or their own communities. These materials can be used in developing a wide-range of reports and projects.

Material from the Census Bureau can be incorporated into Social Studies units. Information on crime, divorce rates, suicide, drug abuse, wealth, and poverty, are just some of the types of information that can be obtained. Data provided through the Census Bureau can be used to develop graphs and charts in Mathematics classes.

United States Census Bureau
    http://www.census.gov

This is the home page for the Census Bureau. It will lead you to a wide-range of demographic information, as well as provide opportunities to ask experts questions related to census data.

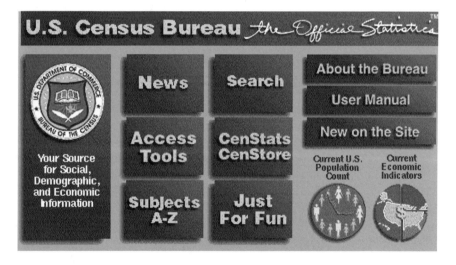

MONITOR DISEASES

| Social Studies | Science | Mathematics | Language Arts |

Information about diseases such as AIDS is vital for students to obtain. Different Internet sites provide outstanding compilations of statistical data, as well as descriptions of specific diseases and their characteristics. Information from these sources can be used for class discussions and reports.

This activity is an excellent starting point for Social Studies classes concerned with contemporary issues, as well as health classes discussing disease control and prevention. An outstanding data source on health issues worldwide is:

Global Health Network
http://info.pitt.edu/HOME/GHNet/GHNet.html

The United States Centers for Disease Control is an excellent source for a wide-range of information on health issues such as AIDS.

Centers for Disease Control
http://www.cdc.gov/cdc.html

HEALTHY DIETS

Social Studies	Mathematics	Language Arts

Have students collect information on developing good eating habits and diets. Have them compile information on appropriate weight, vitamins, benefits of exercise, and related topics. Ask them to present their research in the form of written and oral reports, and bulletin board and poster presentations.

An excellent activity for courses in basic Science, as well as Health Education and Home Economics. A good source for information on nutrition and developing good eating habits is:

International Food Information Council
http://ificinfo.health.org

VOLCANOES

Social Studies	Science

Volcanoes and other geology topics have Internet sites. Students can visit these sites to learn more about volcanology and other aspects of geology.

Activities involving volcanoes provide one of the most interesting ways of introducing students to the fundamentals of Geology. NASA sponsors the Volcano World site, which provides extensive data on volcano activity throughout the world, as well as information about working as a geologist.

Volcano World
     http://volcano.und.nodak.edu

ANATOMY LESSONS

Science

Students can visit various anatomy sites to obtain highly detailed anatomical drawings and information. Projects can focus on specific parts of the body such as the ear, heart, or brain.

This activity is ideally suited for units in Biology and Health education. For example, the following site includes anatomically detailed 3-D pictures of the male and female human body. It is an outstanding site for any students or teachers interested in human biology and anatomy.

The Visible Human Project
     http://www.nnlm.nlm.nih.gov/scr/scnn/
     9501/9501vhp.html

FRANK LLOYD WRIGHT

Social Studies	Humanities
Mathematics	Language Arts

For students interested in architecture, the Internet provides a rich source of information. Many different sites are available, including ones on famous architects such as Frank Lloyd Wright.

Information on the history of architecture, as well as famous architects, fits nicely into Social Studies and Humanities courses. Biographies of architects, histories of buildings, and so on can be linked to different parts of the curriculum.

For detailed resources on the life and work of one of America's greatest architects, visit:

Frank Lloyd Wright Architecture Exhibit
http://flw.badgernet.com:2080

HUMAN RIGHTS

Social Studies	Humanities	Language Arts

The Internet is an ideal place to exchange information about human rights issues. Many sites can be found that will provide students with valuable information. Students may wish to follow human rights abuses in certain countries, or to assist in the protection of specific individuals.

This activity is obviously an excellent one for classes where issues of social justice are emphasized. A unit on ethics could use a site such as this in very interesting ways. The Global Democracy Network has information on political prisoners and human rights issues around the world.

Global Democracy Network
http:/www.gdn.org/

VISIT THE SISTINE CHAPEL

Social Studies   Humanities   Language Arts

The Internet is an ideal place to see the great art of the world. Students can research major works such as the Sistine Chapel. Assignments can include writing about the chapel and its art for an art encyclopedia, creating a guided tour of the chapel, or an essay on Michelangelo's life.

This activity fits Art classes and Social Studies classes extremely well. Students can study Michelangelo's work as an art project, deal with his biography in a Social Studies context, and so on.

The following site contains over 300 images from the Sistine Chapel, as well as extensive information on its background and history.

Sistine Chapel
   http://www.christusrex.org/www1/sistine/
   0-Tour.html

STUDY WEATHER

Science   Mathematics

The weather is all around us and is one of the most interesting subjects for students to study. Comparative information, graphing, and chart-making are natural activities for students to pursue.

These are excellent activities for general science courses. A jumping off point for dozens of Internet sites dealing with weather is:

Meteorology Links
   http://www.ugems.psu.edu/~owens/
   WWW_Virtual_Library/

RESEARCH BIOGRAPHIES

| Social Studies Science Humanities |
| Mathematics Language Arts |

Biographical dictionaries found on the Internet provide extensive information about the lives of important individuals. Have students choose a favorite figure and discover as much as they can.

Biographies of this type can be used in almost any field, not just for Social Studies. Students can find information on famous scientists, mathematicians, and literary figures, as well as famous figures in other disciplines. A biographical dictionary with over 16,000 entries is found at:

Biographical Dictionary
    http://www.tiac.net/users/parallax

TRACK LEGISLATION

| Social Studies |

Legislation can be tracked by going to various Internet sites.

Have students in Social Studies and Civic courses track current legislation through Congress. Thomas is a major source for information on the federal and state government. Major Congressional legislation, as well as the *Congressional Record* are available at this site:

Thomas
    http://thomas.loc.gov

5

MODEL INTERNET LESSON PLANS

CREATING LESSON PLANS FOR THE INTERNET

There is a tendency, when you first start to explore the Internet and the World Wide Web, to wander all over the place. It's so easy to do so. Going online is a bit like going into a wonderful new bookstore. There are fascinating materials on art, science, cooking, family history, religion, mathematics—the whole world seems to be laid out before you. "What do I want to learn about?" " Where should I go?" "What can I find to use with my students?"

Wandering the Internet is great fun, but eventually you need to focus on how it can help you. If you find it a bit overwhelming, think about how you would approach a bookstore or library. Just because there are thousands of fascinating books, doesn't mean you try to read and use them all at once. It's the same with the Internet.

What you need to do is develop a strategy. "What do I want to accomplish using the Internet?" "How can it help me with my student's specific curricular needs?"

This chapter helps you do more than just browse the Internet. It shows you how to effectively tap into the Internet and its resources and how to create lesson plans that you can use in your own classroom. While creating a lesson plan is nothing new for most of the readers of this book, figuring out how to integrate effectively the Internet and the World Wide Web into your teaching is probably new experience.

GETTING STARTED: A MODEL FOR AN ONLINE LESSON PLAN

Creating a good lesson plan is a systematic, step-by-step process. It involves thinking through these seven points:

- Title
- Purpose or Objective
- Competencies to be Met (District and/or State)
- Theme
- Materials
- Design/Procedure
- Evaluation

WHAT IS THE TITLE OF YOUR PROJECT?

Develop a title that is as clear and straightforward as possible.

WHAT IS THE PURPOSE OR OBJECTIVE OF YOUR LESSON?

What is the purpose of your lesson—what is its goal or objective? What are you trying to achieve?

WHAT COMPETENCIES ARE TO BE MET?

How does your lesson fit into District or State Curriculum Competencies or Standards? When designing the purpose of your project it's important to start with the graduation standards and outcomes required by your local school district and state. These standards are required in almost every public school and many private schools as well. Even though there isn't a national curriculum in the United States, curriculum guidelines are fairly standard across the country. This is a result of the influence of national accreditation groups, textbook publishers, and a general agreement on what students need to learn when. For example, addition and subtraction need to be learned before multiplication and division so they are taught early in the curriculum.

WHAT IS THE THEME OR SUBJECT OF YOUR LESSON?

What is the theme or subject of your lesson plan? What is it that holds the lesson together?

WHAT MATERIALS WILL YOU NEED FOR YOUR LESSON?

What materials do you need for your lesson? Does it require more than just access to the Internet? Do students need specific books, writing materials, and so forth?

WHAT IS THE DESIGN OR PROCEDURE FOR YOUR LESSON?

What is the design or set of procedures your lesson should follow? Lay out the lesson step-by-step.

HOW ARE STUDENTS TO BE EVALUATED?

How will students be evaluated in terms of the work they have completed?

This outline is intended as a framework to help you begin to organize and develop your own Internet lesson plans. It can be used at many different grade levels and can be modified to suit your own particular needs. Let's actually use it for developing a curriculum about endangered animals for middle school students.

ENDANGERED ANIMALS IN THE FLORIDA EVERGLADES: AN INTERNET AND WORLD WIDE WEB CURRICULUM

In the Dade County Public Schools, fourth grade students are expected, as part of their work in Social Studies, to develop an understanding of Florida geography and culture. This includes an awareness of the Everglades, their location, their role in the region's ecology, and the plants and animals that live in them.

First a title is needed for the unit:

1. Endangered Animals and the Florida Everglades: A Middle School Social Studies Unit

Next you should go online and find out what resources are available on the Internet for both you and your students to use. When using the search engine Infoseek over 7,000 sites came up. I just need four or five good ones to start with. After reviewing about 100 listings and actually visiting 25 to 30 sites, I decided that the following would be good ones to use with fourth graders. I placed them in the bookmark section of my browser in a special Everglades electronic folder so that I could easily return to them. In addition, my students can easily find them by going to the bookmark list, which is easy to install on their computer.

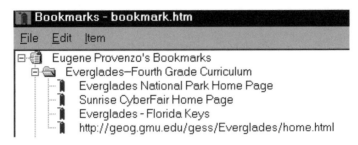

Bookmark file and web sites as displayed in Netscape. For a description of Everglades National Park, see:

National Park Service, Everglades National Park
http://www.nps.gov/ever/

A guide to the Florida Keys with extensive material on the Everglades, including pictures can be found at:

Florida Keys On-Line Guide
http://www.florida-keys.fl.us/everglad.htm

A college curriculum at George Mason University in Virginia, which includes extensive background about the Everglades, as well as links to other Everglades Web sites, is found at:

The River of Grass
http://geog.gmu.edu/gess/Everglades/
home.html

This is Sunrise Middle School's award winning Cyber Fair 96 project "Discover the Florida Everglades." Sunrise Middle School is located in Fort Lauderdale, Florida, and is one of 35 middle schools in Broward County. The project was assembled by a student team. It has extensive links to Everglade-related sites and a great deal of useful information of its own.

Sunrise Middle School's Cyber Fair Home Page
   http://www.fau.edu/divdept/coe/tea/
   cyberfair.html

2. Purpose or Objective:

The purpose of this unit is help students learn about the Everglades, what it's like as a natural environment and its importance to the ecology of the region. In addition, the unit will help students identify current environmental problems, as well as learn about species of animals and plants found in Florida—particularly those that are endangered.

3. Competencies to be Met (District and/or State):

Specifically Grade Four Social Studies competencies will be met under the subsection 4.1 Geographic Understanding. Related skills in science, language arts, and computer literacy will also be achieved.

4. Theme:

The Everglades as part of Florida's environment—its importance to the economy and ecology of the region.

5. Materials:

+ Computer with Internet access to Everglades data bases.
+ High quality printer
+ Pen and paper
+ Bulletin Board

6. Design/Procedure:

This curriculum will take a week to complete. It is expected that students will work on it using three computers on a rotating basis. Total time spent will be between 3 and 4 hours including introduction, discussion, research, and reporting. Students will work in pairs to collect information. On Day 1 (Monday) the instructor will introduce the Everglades unit. Descriptions of the Everglades, why we need to be concerned about it, and our environment will be introduced. Discussion will focus on the class assembling a bulletin board exhibit on the Everglades and endangered animals. Each student will be expected to collect information on a single animal (Florida Panther, Glades Deer, etc.) and how it is threatened. Using the bookmarked sites on the class's computers, they will collect information and photographs. They will then each write a 150-word report with an illustration. Reports will be presented on Thursday afternoon. They will be posted on the bulletin board on Friday and the display will be left up through the end of the following week. Students will have the option of including their reports and pictures in their online portfolio and Web page, although they will need to understand that because of space limitations, they may need to remove one of their earlier projects.

Supplemental activities could include writing to government officials about the needs of endangered animals or creating a brief book on an endangered animal. Students could also set up e-mail exchanges with students in other parts of the country dealing with endangered animals and environmental concerns.

7. Evaluation:

Reports will be evaluated for the clarity of their writing and the thoroughness of their research. Extra credit will be given to students who are interested in drawing pictures of their endangered animal.

The basic model used here can be adapted for almost any subject matter. Next is an example that uses Alexander Graham Bell that shows how the same curriculum model can be used for an eighth grade Social Studies unit on famous Americans and their contributions to American society.

ALEXANDER GRAHAM BELL (1847–1992)

The study of different historical figures is common throughout all levels of the curriculum. The Internet provides invaluable biographical sources. The following curriculum is designed for use in eighth grade American history. It can be adapted for use in senior high school American history classes as well.

1. Alexander Graham Bell—A Biographical Exploration for Eighth Grade American History

Alexander Graham Bell is best known for his invention of the telephone in 1876. He was born March 3, 1847, in Edinburgh, Scotland. After attending high school and college he went to Canada with his father in 1870. In 1872, he moved to the United States where he was a professor of deaf education at Boston University. His interests included the transmission of sound by electricity. He was particularly interested in developing an electrical hearing aid that could be used by deaf people. It was his experiments in this area that led to the invention of the telephone.

Bell demonstrated his invention publicly for the first time at the Philadelphia Centennial Exhibition. The exhibition was the first World's Fair held in the United States and was an important part of the country's 100th anniversary celebration. His demonstration took place on Sunday, June 25, 1876.

Go online to find out what sources are available on Bell. Here are some you might find helpful.

Begin with biographical background on Bell. An excellent place to begin is:

Who Was Alexander Graham Bell?
   http://www.att.com:80/attlabs/brainspin/alexbell/

This site, which is sponsored by AT&T looks at Bell as "Teacher," "Tinkerer," and "Inventor." Other sites, you might want to explore for biographical information include:

Fitzgerald Studio
   http://www.fitzgeraldstudio.com/core.html

Fitzgerald Studio, a Canadian CD-ROM developer, has created an excellent historical CD on Alexander Graham Bell. Much of it is available on the Web and provides students with an excellent historical background on Bell.

The American Experience (Alexander Graham Bell)
   http://www.pbs.org:80/wgbh/pages/amex/
   technology/telephone/mabell.html

The PBS program *The American Experience* dedicated one of its episodes to Bell and his work. This site includes information on ordering the original program, as well curriculum guides to use with it. An extensive historical site provides useful information on Bell.

The Telephone History Web Site
   http://www.cybercomm.net/~chuck/phones.html

The Telephone History Web Site is an excellent jumping off place to explore all aspects of the history of the telephone.
   An excellent general source on Bell and his work is:

Alexander Graham Bell's Path to the Telephone
   http://jefferson.village.virginia.edu/~meg3c/id/
   albell/homepage.html

A very good source for historical background on Bell, particularly in the context of his work in deaf education, is:

American Federation of the Blind
   http://www.igc.apc.org/afb/index.html

2. Purpose or Objective

Figures such as Bell, the history of the telephone, or his experimental work on flight, are subjects that are inherently interesting to students. The purpose of this curriculum unit is to have students collect materials on and to learn about Alexander Graham Bell, his life, and history.

3. Competencies to be Met (District and/or State)

Historical content for the history of invention and American history will be met through this curriculum unit. In addition, competencies related to skills in science, language arts, and computer literacy will also be achieved.

4. Theme

Alexander Graham Bell—his life and inventions.

5. Materials

♦ Computer with Internet access to databases on Alexander Graham Bell and related topics.

♦ High quality printer

♦ Pen and paper

♦ Bulletin board

6. Design Procedure

This curriculum can be limited to one or two class sessions, or extended over several weeks. If students have study hall time, or access to computers at home or in a local library, the time spent on the project can be quite extensive.

One organizing approach that can be taken is to have students conduct a scavenger hunt and assemble a bulletin board and timeline of Bell's life and work.

The instructor may want to give students visual and informational teasers to get them started looking for material on Bell. For example, look at the illustration on the next page. Can you guess what it is?

It's a Tetrahedral Kite—a lighter than air machine designed to carry the weight of a person. The shape was triangular with a fourth side open underneath. It consisted of small silk cells stitched together to connect a lightweight wooden structure. The idea was Bell's, whose aim was to be the first to build a kite capable of lifting a man and then to construct a kite aerodynamically sound, with room in its tetrahedral corpus for a passenger and an engine.

Have students find illustrations of this invention of Bell's by visiting sites such as:

Alexander Graham Bell
   http://www.chatsubo.com:80/fitzgerald/bell/
   inventor.html#tetra

The Alexander Graham Bell Institute
   http://bell.uccb.ns.ca/

"Mr. Watson, come here—I want you." were the first words transmitted by telephone. On March 10, 1876, while setting up his equipment, Bell accidentally spilled battery acid on his trousers and called out to his assistant. Watson was waiting on the other end of the telephone circuit on another floor of the building when he heard the call. As a starter for this exploration, ask students to try to discover by going online, what were the first words that were spoken over the telephone.

In addition to creating a bulletin board, students can write individual essays on Bell and his inventions and present oral reports on their findings.

7. Evaluation

Students will be evaluated on the clarity of their presentation and the thoroughness of their research.

MODELS FOR CREATING YOUR OWN CURRICULUMS ONLINE

As you become more experienced using the Internet, you may decide to put together your own Web site, including lesson plans. Chapter 10 describes setting up your own Web site. Included below is information about the Art Across Cultures Curriculum, a collaboration between the Department of Teaching and Learning, School of Education and the Lowe Art Museum at the University of Miami. We are in the process of creating an online, or cyberspace, tour of key pieces from the Museum's main collections. This tour also includes curriculum materials for use in Grades K-3 and 4–8, as well as links to museum and educational sites of related interest.

You can reach the home page of the Lowe Art museum at:

Lowe Art Museum, University of Miami
http://www.lowemuseum.org/par.htm

or the School of Education's home page at the Univeristy of Miami at:

School of Education, University of Miami
http://www.education.miami.edu

The Art Across Cultures Curriculum draws on the six major regional and historical collections included in the Lowe Art Museum: The Art of Europe; The Art of the Americas; The Art of Native North America; The Art of the Ancient Americas;

The Art of Asia; and The Art of Africa. The curriculum model and outline is essentially the same as that used in the curriculums on the Everglades and Alexander Graham Bell discussed earlier.

Tom Dughi, a secondary English teacher, put together the following curriculum as his contribution to the Art of the Americas section of the curriculum. It is based on James Rosenquist's pop art print *F-111*.

LESSON PLAN FOR JAMES ROSENQUIST'S *F-111*

PLAN OBJECTIVES

Get students to identify and analyze use of images, symbols, and metaphors in a work of art, and to make thematic connections among a work's various images, symbols, and metaphors. Practice writing a thesis-driven essay.

PLAN TOPIC

Media Images in James Rosenquist's *F-111*

SUBJECT AREA

English or Art

GRADE LEVEL

Grades 8–9

TIME ALLOTTED

One 40-minute class period + 30–45-minute homework assignment

INSTRUCTIONAL CONTENT/PROCEDURES/ TECHNOLOGY ACTIVITY

1. Bring up Lowe Museum image *of F-111* on class computer or projection system.

2. Give a 5-minute introduction to Pop Art and James Rosenquist. Focus on the fact that he was a billboard painter, on his interest in u sing media

images in his artworks, and, if desired, on his opposition to the Vietnam War.

3. 20-minute discussion: First, get students to identify different images in the work and to describe *how* they are painted. Then have them discuss where the artist might have found such images; how his use of images in this painting makes the viewer see them in a new way; whether they are being used as symbols or metaphors, and if so, of what. Finally, have them discuss how the images are thematically connected. Some specific suggestions of images to focus on: (a) the spaghetti, painted an artificial orange color like something out of a can or (even more artificial) like a billboard image of something out of a can; (b) the premixed cake with little pennants listing the vitamins; (c) the Firestone tire with sharp treads and visible brand name; (d) the cheery little girl under a sleek art deco hair-dryer, which in the context of the picture looks like the nosecone of a missile; (e) the mushroom cloud topped with a multicolor beach umbrella—the metaphor of a nuclear umbrella made frighteningly literal; (f) the F-111 itself, which runs the length of the whole painting (ask students why the image of the F-111 is so central?)

4. 15-minute workshop: Students brainstorm thesis statements for a brief essay on the topic: What is the central theme of Rosenquist's *F-111*?

5. Homework assignment: Students write their essays (150–200 words), developing their thesis statements with specific examples of images from the painting.

6. Optional technology activity: Students visit other Web sites for James Rosenquist and/or Pop Art (see below)

INSTRUCTIONAL / TECHNOLOGICAL AIDS & MATERIALS

Class computer or projection system, wordprocessors or pen and pencil for writing essay

(Optional) Handout on Pop Art and James Rosenquist

Internet resources:

Pop Art
    http://www.suu.edu/WebPages/Museum
    Galler/Art101/popart.html

A brief listing of some of the main characteristics of Pop Art along with brief material on artists including Rosenquist.

James Rosenquist
    http://www.fi.muni.cz/~toms/PopArt/
    Biographies/rosenquist.html

General overview of Rosenquist's work and art.

National Gallery of Art
    http://www.nga.gov/cgi-bin/pbio?230980

Brief biography of Rosenquist with an introduction to his work as an artist.

ASSESSMENT/EVALUATION

Assess classroom responses and discussion.

Grade student essays.

There are many other curriculum models that can be adapted and used other than those outlined above. A different type of model involves the use of "Curriculum Exploration Cards."

CURRICULUM EXPLORATION CARDS

A useful model recently developed by the author involves "curriculum cards," which are model lesson plans that can be explored by students on an individual basis or used as part of group classroom activities. An example of this type of curriculum is provided in the following unit on American Slavery. Adopt this model for use at your own grade level and in ways that meet your own curriculum needs.

American Slavery

Student Objective: Your objective is to learn about the experience of slavery in the United States. You will do this by exploring oral history accounts, photographs, and public documents.

You can explore the oral history accounts of slaves who told the story of their lives to researchers during the 1930s. These slave narratives can be found online at:

American Memory (Library of Congress)
http://lcweb2.loc.gov/amhome.html
University of Virginia Hypertext Library
http://xroads.virginia.edu?~HYPER/wpa/
wpahome.html

You can look at photographs such as the one that shows the Slave Market in St. Augustine, Florida. These photographs can be found at:

American Memory Collection Search Engine
http://lcweb2.loc.gov/ammem/amframe.html

*Use words like *slaves, slavery,* and *slave narratives* with the search engine to find related materials.

You can look at documents such as the Emancipation Proclamation.

The Emancipation Proclamation was issued on January 1, 1863, as the American Civil War entered its third year. It declared "that all persons held as slaves within the rebel states of the South are, and henceforward shall be free." The Emancipation Proclamation stands as one of the most important documents in our nation's history. You can actually see it online by visiting the National Archives.

Emancipation Proclamation (National Archives and Record Administration)
   http://www.nara.gov:80/exhall/featured-document/eman/emanproc.html

Use these questions to guide your exploration:

1. How was slavery a cruel and inhumane experience? (Slave Narratives, University of Virginia; American Memory Collection)

2. Did the Emancipation Proclamation free all of the slaves in the United States? (Emancipation Proclamation)

3. Find a photograph of a slave that tells you something about what they experienced as people under slavery (American Memory Collection and National Archives)

4. Can you find evidence in your explorations of why slavery was such a cruel a thing to do to people? (Slave Narratives, University of Virginia; American Memory Collection)

Use these activities to show what you have learned.

1. Create a bulletin board of photographs and narratives that will help people better understand what the experience of slavery was like.

2. Imagine that you have been transported back to the 19th century and are a reporter who has been asked to write a newspaper article on the Emancipation Proclamation and the freeing of the slaves. What would be the headline for your article? What would be the main point included in it?

6

ELECTRONIC MAIL

WHAT IS E-MAIL?

Electronic mail or e-mail is one of the most common uses of the Internet. E-mail is similar to regular mail in that one person sends a note to the other. The big difference is that e-mail is done electronically and messages are delivered almost instantaneously, compared to postal services ("snail mail"), which can take days, or even weeks.

What is e-mail?

"E-mail" means electronic mail. It is a messaging system that allows Internet users to send messages back and forth much like the postal system.

What is snail mail?

Snail mail is the name e-mail users have given to traditional, slower mail sent by postal

---

There are many possible uses of e-mail in classrooms. Students can communicate with one another, with friends in other schools, or with people who live across the country or overseas. They can sign on to mailing lists for specific discussion topics or interests.

What is a mailing list?

A mailing list, in the context of e-mail, is an electronic list of addresses. Mailing lists make it possible for a single message to be addressed to many people at once. This function is particularly helpful when sharing information with a group, or in getting people to work together on committees, and so on.

E-mail has many advantages over traditional mail, including:

♦ E-mail is delivered instantly.

♦ Documents can be attached to e-mail.

♦ E-mail costs very little to use compared to long distances telephone calls, or even to the postal service and overnight delivery companies.

♦ Messages can be sent to multiple addresses at once.

♦ Group discussions can occur using e-mail.

♦ Unlike the telephone, e-mail does not require its recipient to be present to accept a message. Differences between world time zones and in schedules become less of a problem for people who want to communicate with one another.

Most e-mail consists of text, although sound and visual images are being included in more messages.

In many respects, e-mail operates like regular mail. There is a sender, a recipient, an address for the receiver, and a return address for the sender. E-mail messages are deliberately kept short. Abbreviations are frequently used such as: CUL (see you later), BTW (by the way), FYI (for your information), FYA (for your amusement), IMHO (in my humble opinion), IOW (in other words), and TIA (thanks in advance). Emoticons, or "smileys," are also used in e-mail to express feelings. These are created by combining different punctuation marks (be sure to look at them sideways). Popular symbols include:

:-)   smile or happiness

:-(a frown

;-)   an inside joke or whimsy

E-mail has a set of customs associated with it known as "netiquette." These customs involve the "proper" way to write something, and so on. A discussion of netiquette is included in Chapter 7, "Establishing an Acceptable Use Policy for Your School."

ANATOMY OF AN E-MAIL MESSAGE

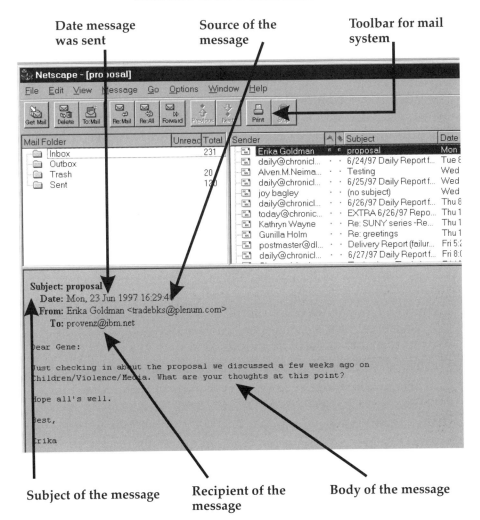

Date message was sent

Source of the message

Toolbar for mail system

Subject of the message

Recipient of the message

Body of the message

A good way to encourage students to use e-mail is to have them send an e-mail message to the White House. Have them connect to:

> **White House Correspondence**
> **http://www.whitehouse.gov/WH/Mail/html/**
> **Mail_President.html**

This site provides a graphical user-interface (GUI, pronounced "gooey" in computerese) for sending e-mail messages to the White House. It can provide a valuable writing exercise for students by having them go through a step-by-step writing experience including Organization, Address, Purpose, Topic, Affiliation, and Subject.

What is a graphical interface?

A graphical interface is the visual information a user interacts with on a computer screen. Graphical interfaces are designed for ease of use.

ELECTRONIC BULLETIN BOARDS

Electronic bulletin boards are the town squares on the Internet. They provide a place for people to post messages for others to find. Bulletin boards are a great place to connect with people who have similar interests. Suppose you are interested in finding innovative science curriculums to use with your students. You can leave a message on an electronic bulletin board explaining what you are interested in locating. You will discover very quickly that there are people there with the answers you need.

What is an electronic bulletin board?

An electronic bulletin board is a place where people post messages and announcements that can be shared with others. Unlike e-mail, the messages are not addressed to a specific individual.

DISCUSSION GROUPS

A discussion group lets people with mutual interests interact and exchange e-mail and documents. A list of Web-based discussion groups, along with information on how to subscribe to educational discussion groups, can be found at:

USENET Discussion Groups
   http://k12.cnidr.org:90/usenets.html

Chat programs allow the exchange of messages back and forth as part of an online conversation. As many as six people can participate on a chat line. A good source is:

Mirabilis
   http://www.mirabilis.com

What is a chat program?

A chat program is an electronic discussion program that allows people to interact and respond to each other in real-time online.

FILE TRANSFER

E-mail programs make it possible to send computer files, including graphic and text files, to remote locations. On net browsers such as Netscape, this is done by attachments to the e-mail letter using the e-mail function of the program. For more information about e-mail file attachments visit online:

E-Mail Web Resources
   http://andrew2.andrew.cmu.edu/cyrus/email/

7

ESTABLISHING AN ACCEPTABLE USE POLICY FOR YOUR SCHOOL

PROBLEMS ARISING FROM USING THE INTERNET IN SCHOOLS

Throughout this book I have emphasized that a principal benefit of the Internet and the World Wide Web is that they bring the world to the child. Through access to a multitude of sites from around the world, students can obtain information and communicate with people in ways that make learning a whole new experience.

Yet, giving students such access to information and ideas is not without danger. The Internet does not discriminate on the basis of age. Children can enter adult chat rooms, view pornographic bulletin boards, or connect to sources of information that may not be considered appropriate by their parents or the communities in which they live.

Should a ninth grader who thinks that she is gay and lives in a rural western community with fundamentalist religious values, use the Internet to connect to an adult alternative sex bulletin board or chat line? Are you responsible for a student downloading pornographic pictures from the Internet? What do you do if a student plagiarizes a term paper using Internet resources?

In many regards, these are not new problems. School libraries often have materials that students can use inappropriately. Schools are also places where students can meet other individuals who do not meet the approval of their parents or other members of the community. Pornographic magazines and other inappropriate materials have always been passed among students at school.

The difference is that the Internet is a major channel through which these materials and issues circulate. It is important, therefore, that appropriate policies be established for the use of computers and the Internet in the schools. Use policies apply not only to students, but also to faculty, staff, and administrators.

Acceptable use of the Internet operates at a number of different levels. Just as there are rules of proper behavior in church, or at a public lecture or concert, so, too, are there rules of proper behavior on the Internet. These are commonly referred to as "netiquette."

What is netiquette?
> Netiquette are the rules of proper behavior on the Internet.

Probably the best rule to follow, as with etiquette in general, is to treat people in a way that is consistent with how you would like to be treated yourself. The following are a few examples of things to be avoided:

- Typing in ALL CAPS on bulletin boards and chat lines. For many people this is considered the equivalent of shouting.
- Saying things that could damage a person. You don't always know to whom your messages might be forwarded.
- Sending messages with abusive or foul language.
- Clogging people's mailboxes with unnecessary files or overly long messages.

Netiquette guidelines can be found online at:

Arlene Rinaldi, Florida Atlantic University
http://rs6000.adm.fau.edu/faahr/netiquette.html

Some things are actually against the law or border on being illegal on the Internet. Avoid the following at all costs:

- Placing illegal information on the Internet.
- Sending out programs that in any way interfere with the work or operation of another person's system.

Here are some good basics rules that should always be followed by yourself and your students.

- Never harm anyone through your use of a computer.
- Never interfere with someone else's work using a computer.
- Never use a computer to do something illegal.
- Never use illegally obtained software.
- Never use another person's ideas without proper credit.

ESTABLISHING AN ACCEPTABLE USE POLICY

Acceptable use policies are essential to any school system where students go online. Essentially, an acceptable use policy is a contract signed by students, parents, teachers, and administrators whereby they each agree to specific rules on using the Internet and its resources.

What is an acceptable use policy (AUP)?

An agreement signed by students, parents, teachers, and administrators concerning the agreed upon rules for using the Internet in a particular school.

An acceptable use policy includes at least these four elements:

- The policy explains how the Internet is connected to the teaching and learning expected in the classroom. This includes who will have access to the Internet and how access will be managed.

♦ The policy explains student responsibilities while online. This includes a description of Internet etiquette, commonly called "netiquette."

♦ The policy includes the consequences that will result from the violation of the agreement.

♦ The policy is written and agreed to by students and parents, as well as teachers, administrators, and staff.

For information on acceptable use policies and problems of going online, go to:

Harnessing the Power of the Web
http://www.gsn.org/web/tutorial/index.htm

Included in Appendix B are model Acceptable Use policies and permission forms from the Bellingham, Washington, public schools. These are excellent models for most school districts. The Bellingham School District generously allows the modification and use of these documents for nonprofit organizations. If you would like to visit the Bellingham School Districts Home Page for updated versions of these documents, go online to:

Bellingham School District
http://www.bham.wednet.edu

PROTECTING STUDENTS USING THE INTERNET

Keeping students from misusing or accessing inappropriate material on the Internet is just one of the concerns parents and teachers have for their children and students. Another issue has to do with their safety. In the past year or so, there have been several well-publicized incidents involving children being contacted by adults via the Internet and subsequently lured away from their homes.

Children should be warned not to provide strangers with their photograph, phone number, or address over the Internet. They need to understand that someone who seems friendly on the Internet may, in fact, not have their best interests at heart.

Useful child safety information is provided at these sites:

Child Safety and Censorship on the Net
   http://www.voicenet.com/~cranmer/
   censorship.html
Child Safety Online
   http://www.omix.com/magid/child.safety.
   online.html

Censorship
Freedom of Speech
Child Safety on the Internet

**There are many excellent sites on the Internet that
deal with child safety and censorship issues**

Information on how to electronically block children's access to inappropriate sections of the Internet and Acceptable Use Policies for children and parents can be found at:

Safe Surf Home Page
   http://www.safesurf.com/index.html

Different companies provide software to block inappropriate Internet sites for students. CyberPatrol (1-800-638-1639) costs $29.95 and includes a free subscription to and automatic update (every 10 days) of *Cybernot*, a continually updated list of inappropriate Web sites for young children. Other programs are Surf Watch (1-800-458-6600) and *Cyber Sitter* (1-800-388-2761). These programs are not foolproof. Students always have the potential to find inappropriate material if they try hard enough. Art and photography exhibits, anatomy and literature sites, chat rooms, and bulletin boards with nontraditional names and inappropriate material can always be found. Having an effective Acceptable Use Policy is important, therefore, because it places the responsibility for accessing appropriate materials on the user, rather than on the school system.

HELPING PARENTS UNDERSTAND THE INTERNET

Using the Internet opens up a world to children they would not otherwise have access to. By implementing free and creative use of the Internet in your school, you may be opening yourself up to criticisms that the Internet is an inappropriate place for students to explore.

Make sure that parents are completely aware of how your school is using the Internet. Many parents are not computer literate. Have an open house to show them how the Internet works. Take them to selected sites and show them how their children are using these sites as part of their schoolwork.

Explain to parents about the precautions your school is taking to protect their children when they go online. Make sure that they understand what an acceptable use policy is and how it works.

Finally, remember that many of the problems faced in using the Internet are not new, but have been dealt with by educators in the past. What is critical is that you be consistent, ethical, and keep the best interests of your students and the local community in mind.

8

LEARNING ABOUT OTHERS THROUGH THE INTERNET

CONNECTING CLASSROOMS AND CULTURES

In *Brave New Schools,* Jim Cummins and Dennis Sayers chronicle the efforts of the pioneer educators Celestin Freinet and Rene Daniel to have their students share writing and other materials as part of a cultural exchange. Freinet began his work in a one-room school in the French Maritime Alps in 1920. There he developed three complementary teaching techniques that eventually lead to long distance educational partnerships and what became known as the Modern School Movement. (Cummins and Sayers, pp. 123–125)

The first technique developed by Freinet was to take his students on "learning walks" through their village and local neighborhoods. Students would gather information about community life that would become the basis for subsequent classroom activities. As a followup to these walks students would then create "free texts," which would be turned into "pre-texts"—documents that addressed problems or needs in their local communities.

As a result of their community-based walks, students became involved in projects such as building a new village fountain and constructing a small hydroelectric dam on a local stream. Initially, reports were collected in a folder. To more widely disseminate these reports, Freinet introduced his second technique, which involved students typesetting their reports and distributing them among themselves and their families and friends. (*Ibid.,* p. 125)

The third technique introduced by Freinet was to have students establish interschool networks. This was originally done with Rene Daniel, a teacher in neighboring province. In Octo-

ber 1924, they exchanged "culture packages" and writing between their students.

The model that eventually evolved had two teachers in distant schools matched in a partnership. Cultural packages were
exchanged between classes, along with examples of individual
student work. Eventually Freinet's program lead to team-
teaching partnerships among 10,000 schools throughout the
world. (*Ibid.*, p. 126)

French teachers were eventually given free postage by the
government to pursue their exchange projects. Freinet's model
emphasized the development of cooperative learning models
and the development of a broadly based and experiential cultural and social literacy. Freinet schools continue to operate today in France and around the world. For schools using their
model of curriculum, computers and the Internet are extraordinary resources. Using the Internet, students can exchange "cultural packages," write letters to one another, and work together on collaborative projects.

HARNESSING THE INTERNET TO UNDERTAKE GLOBAL STUDENT EXCHANGES

The Internet is an ideal place for students to undertake
global exchanges. Many different programs are underway that
allow students to link themselves to other schools and cultures
throughout the world.

A good place to start is the Dewey Web, sponsored by the
University of Michigan, which has as its purpose increasing
global awareness. Go online to:

> **The Dewey Web**
>   http://ics.soe.umich.edu

The Dewey Web will provide background on various projects such as *Wild Adventures: The Journey North*, which linked
classrooms to scientists and explorers, as well as other schools
and locations. *The Route 12 Project*, which runs along Route 12
from Detroit, Michigan, to the state of Washington, provided
students with a tour of the sites along the highway, as well as

links to other students living along the thousands of miles over which it runs.

The Global SchoolNet Foundation, formerly known as FREDMail (Free Educational Mail) originated in the mid-1980s with a group of teachers in San Diego who were interested in having their students take advantage of the Internet and be able to exchange information with one another. They sponsor a wide-range of programs involving student and teacher exchanges. Connect to them at:

Global SchoolNet Foundation
http://www.gsn.org

All About Education is a web site that will help teachers, students, and parents set up e-mail exchanges.

All About Education
http://www.shadetree.com/~rplogman/

Kidlink connects students from around the world to exchange information and ideas. Over 60,000 people have participated in their programs. To introduce themselves on the system, students have to answer four questions (1. Who am I? 2. What do I want to be when I grow up? 3. How do I want the world to be better when I grow up? 4. What can I do to make this happen?). Here is an example of a student response from Grahamstown, South Africa:

1. MY name is luthando mqulwana and I am from Alice (S.A.) my home language is XHOSA and I was born in SOUTH AFRICA. I go to college at ST ANDREW"S COLLEGE (S.A.). I am 14, 3 years old and I am in std 8. Since I went to school I have only been to four school but I have never been expelled but am a rebel in my sort of way. You must enjoy life while you can.

2. When I grow up I want to be a doctor and I think I will have to put a lot of effort to be that.

3. I would like everyone to live in peace to love each other and care for each other. This is the world God created for us so we must take care of it hope that happens.

4. I want to pray that happens and I hope you do that too.

You can connect to Kidlink at:

Kidlink
   http://www.kidlink.org

MUDs (MULTIPLE USER DUNGEONS) AND MOOs (MUD OBJECT ORIENTED)

Another very different way of having students connect to other people is through MUDs (Multiple User Dungeons) and MOOs (Mud Object Oriented). MUDs and MOOs are among the most interesting developments on the Internet. These are imaginary adventure games created in online computer databases.

MOOS are slightly more sophisticated than MUDS. They are less text-oriented and involve more use of graphics.

What is a MUD?

   MUD is an acronym for Multiple User Dungeon. These are imaginary adventure games resident on computer networks.

What is a MOO?

   MOO is an acronym for Mud Object Oriented. It is a technically more sophisticated MUD.

MUDs can trace their roots back to participatory adventure games like *Dungeons and Dragons*. Howard Rheingold describes MUDs as, "imaginary worlds in computer databases where people use words and programming languages to improvise melodramas, build worlds and all the objects in them, solve puzzles, invent amusements and tools, compete for prestige and power, gain wisdom, seek revenge, indulge greed and lust and violent impulses."

MUDs were first introduced in England in 1980. By the early 1990s there were nearly 200 such games underway on the Internet, based on 19 different programming languages.

MUDs allow the user to enter into a highly complex gaming scenario, to define a character for themselves, and to endow their character with specific characteristics and powers. Participants in MUDs can also endow objects with powers. A chair can talk. When a wall is touched it can release the solution to a puzzle. A tree can have consciousness. Locations such as castles, dungeons, or spaceships created by a player in a MUD can be explored by other people participating in the game.

In his novella *True Names*, Vernor Vinge describes a "game" played on a national computer network that would seem to be the ultimate evolution of the MUDs. The game players in *True Names* construct their characters in highly sophisticated visual and auditory simulations. They are not bound by the laws of the known physical world. Thus, an individual may be transformed into a dragon or into a monster by invoking a special command or set of spells (that is a programming sequence). They can die within the system and then be reborn.

MUDs and stories like *True Names* suggest that an alternative magical and symbolic world is emerging on the frontiers of the digital revolution. Using an Internet connection, you might want to try to explore these virtual worlds.

Here is a useful addresses to help you get started exploring MUDs and MOOs:

Role-Playing Game Internet Resource Guide
http://www.common.net/~shadow/rpg_index/

9

USEFUL WEB SITES FOR TEACHERS

The World Wide Web is an extremely rich source for teachers. Lesson plans, innovative programs, information about educational exchanges, even graduate instruction can all be found on the Web. What follows is a list of sites that teachers will find particularly useful.

Eye On Education, the publisher of this book, sponsors a Web site with descriptions of innovative programs and practices that have been successfully implemented at elementary, middle, and high schools. A different program is featured each month.

Best Practice of the Month
   http://www.eyeoneducation.com

This site provides information on the annual book award for illustrated children's books.

Caldecott Award
   http://ils.unc.edu/award/chome.html

This is an invaluable basic factbook on world affairs.

CIA World Factbook '95
   http://libfind.unl.edu:2020/alpha/CIA_World_
   Factbook_1991.html

Preschool through high school curriculum materials provided by teachers.

Collaborative Lesson Archive
http://faldo.atmos.uiuc.edu/TUA_Home.html

Extensive information and resources for developing classes in chemistry.

Chemistry Teaching Resources
http://www.anachem.umu.se/eks/pointers.htm

Classroom Connect publishes the best newsletter for K-12 educators dealing with the Internet and World Wide Web. This is a great Web site for finding links to other educational sites, as well as to see what other schools are doing on the Web.

Classroom Connect
http://www.wentworth.com/classroom/

All sorts of resources on major documents from the United States Government. This is the place to go if you want to get a copy of the Constitution or 19th century treaties with different Native American groups.

Clio—The National Archives Information Server
http://gopher.nara.gov:70/

Extensive information and resources for teachers development curriculums involving environmental education.

EE-Link, Environmental Education on the Web
http://es.inel.gov/new/contacts/pubtrng/ed1.html

Links to major educational web sites.

**Educational Bookmarks
http://bush.edu/bookmarks.html**

ERIC is the main index and data source for education information from the U. S. Government. This is the place for teachers and others to visit in order to learn about new educational innovations, current educational trends and innovative lesson plans.

**Educational Resources and Information Center (ERIC)
http://ericir.syr.edu/**

San Francisco's extraordinary children's museum goes online.

**Exploratorium
http://www.exploratorium.edu**

A basic introduction to Hypertext Markup Language.

**An HTML Crash Course for Educators
http://edweb.gsn-org**

Links to dozens of archives of historical information.

History Pointers
http://historyu.cc.ukans.edu/history/
www_history_main.html

This site includes extensive information on current school use of the Internet, as well as useful profiles of schools and their use of the Internet.

Internet Education Statistics
http://k12.cnidr.org/janice_k12/states/
states.html

Extensive educational resources dealing with African studies.

K-12 Electronic Guide for African Resources on the Internet
http://www.sas.upenn.edu/African_Studies/
Home_Page/AFR_GIDE.html

An outstanding collection of Web sites for K-12 educators.

K-12 WWW Links
http://k12.cnidr.org

This site provides extensive links to information sources on music situated on the World Wide Web.

Music Pointers
http://www.oulu.fi/music.html

A Web site devoted to the annual award given to the outstanding children's book of the year.

Newberry Award
http://ils.unc.edu/award/nhome.html

A remarkable set of visual and textual sources on Ancient Greece.

The Perseus Project
  http://www.perseus.tufts.edu

An extensive index to World Wide Web sites.

Planet Earth Home Page
  http://ivory.nosc.mil/planet_earth/Library/
  information.html

An outstanding online information system for exploring topics about space and space exploration.

Spacelink
  http://spacelink.msfc.nasa.gov/

This is an electonic magazine for teachers that provides lesson plans and links to Web sites that can be used in different classroom settings.

Teacher Edition Online
http://www.teachnet.com/teach.html

Excellent resource for using computer technology in classrooms.

Teaching with Technology
http://www.wam.umd.edu/~mlhall/teaching.html

General resources on educational technology.

Reinventing Schools: The Technology is Now!
http://www.nap.edu/nap/online/techngap/

This site, put together by the folks at the Ontario Science Center, will lead you to Web sites involving space, weather, music, and other neat things.

Science Links from the Ontario's Science Center
http://www.osc.on.ca/kiosk/onramp.htm

An excellent online source for all types of economic and business information .

Stat-USA
http://www.stat-usa.gov/

An excellent site for students preparing to take the Scholastic Aptitude Exam (SAT).

The Study Hall
http://rampages.onramp.net/~studyhal/

This site is dedicated to all aspects of urban education. Documents on urban and minority families, innovations in urban education and cultural diversity can all be found here.

Urban Education Web
http://eric-web.tc.columbia.edu

Enter a word you want defined and the definition will be provided. If you don't know how to spell the word, this online dictionary suggests alternative spellings to you.

Webster's Hypertext Dictionary
http://c.gp.cs.cmu.edu:5103/prog/webster

A site for connecting you to virtual exhibitions from around the world.

World Wide Services Connected with Museums
http://www.comlab.ox.ac.uk/archive/other/
museums.html

10

SETTING UP YOUR OWN WEB SITE

School Districts and schools across the country are setting up home pages on the World Wide Web. These home pages provide students a remarkable opportunity to reach out to other parts of the country and around the world. They provide a place to showcase school-based projects and initiatives. *Web66* lists hundreds of school Web sites both in the United States and overseas. The site also has information on setting up Web sites:

Web 66
http://web66.coled.umn.edu

This Web site provides the basic information you need to set up a Web site at your school. Also visit:

WWW Schools Registry
http://hillside.coled.umn.edu/others.html

This is a gateway to the hundreds of North American schools who have servers on the Internet.

HYPERTEXT MARKUP LANGUAGE

Text and graphics are created for a web page using Hypertext Markup Language or HTML. HTML is actual very simple to use. Codes or tags set within angle-brackets (<>) let you modify text and assign special functions to it. The code <center>, for example, put on either side of a piece of text will cause that text to be centered on your Web page.

On the next page is a simple Web page. Beneath it are the HTML codes that make it possible.

There are many good books that will provide you with an introduction to using HTML, as well as Web sites that will keep you updated about new coding commands, changes in the HTML language, and so on.

There are two ways of coding with HTML. You can type the codes into your text or you can use an HTML editor. With the editor you choose a word, sentence, or paragraph, and then click on a command button that changes the appearance of the text. Using an editor this way is almost identical to using a word processor. Editors are being built into Web browsers. In Netscape Navigator Gold, for example, there is an editor built into the system.

Unless they really enjoy programming, most teachers will find that the best way to develop their own Web pages is to use a Web editor. There are many excellent Web editors available that can be bought and used as stand-alone products, including Microsoft's *Front Page*, Adobe's *Page Mill*, Corel's *Web Master Suite*, and Net Object's *Fusion*.

Of course, when you create your own Web page you will probably want to include your own graphics and even sound files. These are advanced functions and can be best learned about by going online to see what other people have done, and to find programs that will help you convert graphics to usable HTML formats.

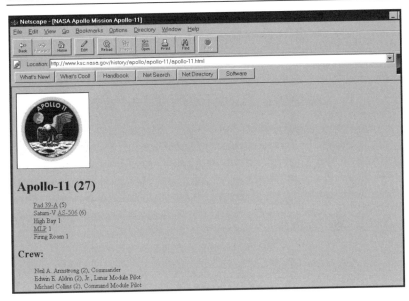

Here is the HTML code for the above NASA Web page.

```
<HTML><HEAD>
<TITLE>NASA Apollo Mission Apollo-11<TITLE>
<meta name="keywords" content="Apollo-11">
</HEAD>
<BODY>
<A HREF = "http://www.ksc.nasa.gov/history/apollo/apollo-
    11/apollo-11-patch.jpg"><IMG SRC = "http://www.ksc.
    nasa.gov/history/apollo/apollo-11/apollo-11-patch-
    small.gif"></A>
<p>
<H1>Apollo-11 (27)</H1>
<DL>
<dd> <AHREF="http://www.ksc.nasa.gov/facilities/
    lc39a.html"Pad 39-A</A> (5)
<dd>Saturn-V <A HREF ="http://www.ksc.nasa.gov/history/
    apollo/apollo-11/apollo-11.html"AS-506</A> (6)
<dd> High Bay 1
<dd> <A HREF="http://www.ksc.nasa.gov/facilities/
    mlp.html"MLP</A> 1
<dd> Firing Room 1
<p></DL>
<H2>Crew:</H2>
<DL>
```

<dd> Neil A. Armstrong (2), Commander
<dd> Edwin E. Aldrin (2), Jr., Lunar Module Pilot
<dd> Michael Collins (2), Command Module Pilot
<p></DL>

CREATING YOUR OWN WEB PAGES

Creating your own Web page either as an individual teacher or with your class is not that difficult. While setting up a stand-alone Web server can be a fairly complicated and expensive task, you can often get space on other people's servers. *Classroom Connect*, for example, which publishes the best Teacher/Internet newsletter currently available, will let you post a home page on its server:

> **Classroom Connect**
> **http://www.classroom.net/classweb/**

To submit your pages, e-mail *Classroom Connect* at: classweb@classroom.net.

To share your Web pages with other individuals on the Internet, they need to be loaded onto a specially set up computer known as a Web server. A Web server lets anyone connected to the Internet browse your Web page.

> **National Center for Supercomputing**
> **http://www.ncsa.uiuc.edu/General/Internet/**
> **WWW/HTMLPrimer.html**

What is a Web server?

A Web server is a computer on which a Web site resides and that can be connected to through the Internet.

STUDENTS AND SCHOOLS ON THE INTERNET

What happens when teachers and students publish on the World Wide Web? What types of things do they write? How can their activities contribute to the mainstream curriculum?

For the rest of this chapter, we look at examples of student and teacher Web sites. Although we provide Internet addresses for all of the sites described, the sites listed here are likely to change as school years come to an end and teachers and students go on to new projects. Consider the examples that I have included as models of what you may want to try to do in your own classroom or school.

To get more up-to-date information, spend some time going through *Web66*'s World Wide Web School Registry. Bookmark your favorite Web sites and return to them at your leisure.

WWW Schools Registry
http://www.acu.edu/dev/makeserver.html

USING THE INTERNET TO SHARE A CLASS FIELD TRIP WITH OTHERS

Yamato Colony Elementary School is a public school located in Livingston, California. Fourth graders in Room P-5 use their school's Web site to post stories, poems, artwork, and other materials that they have created. Samples of the students' work are seen in the following short essays written by them describing their field trip to the Monterey Bay Aquarium on October 17, 1996.

My Trip to the Monterey Bay Aquarium
by Amandeep Kaur

There are many things at the Monterey Bay Aquarium. At the touch pool I touched the sea cucumber. I touched the bay rays three times. They were very soft. When I went upstairs I got to see the sea snakes. One was swimming very fast out of the water and in. One was very long and fat. Outside I saw an otter. It was on the rock. I looked in the telescope. It was very close to me when I looked in the telescope. I saw another one too. It was fun at the Monterey Bay Aquarium.

My Favorite Things at the Monterey Bay Aquarium
by Savanna Burns

Monterey Bay Aquarium has splendid and exciting fish and animals. I liked the touch pool because I got to touch a giant sea cucumber. It felt like a balloon with water inside of the balloon. It looked sharp because it had little spikes on its body. It was an orangish-red color. I also touched a sea urchin. I liked the bat ray pool because the bat rays would sometimes come up and splash you. I felt the bat ray once. The bat ray felt slippery and slimy. The kelp lab was cool. I got to look in four microscopes I liked the kelp lab because I got to touch a white starfish. When I touched the starfish it felt fuzzy. In the middle of the starfish it was pink. Those are my favorite things about Monterey Bay Aquarium.

Yamato County Elementary School
http://members.aol.com/leichert/ycpage.htm

PERSONALIZED STUDENT HOME PAGES FOR AN ENTIRE SCHOOL

Imagine student excitement when students can say that they have a page of their own on the Internet! Students at Hillside Elementary School in Cottage Grove, Minnesota, are doing exactly that by creating their own home pages on their school's Web site. A joint project with the University of Minnesota College of Education and Human Development, student home pages include a personalized drawing, as well as an essay in which each student tells about him or herself and lists an individual e-mail address.

The development of student home pages is part of a larger effort on the part of Hillside students and teachers to expand the curriculum by using the Internet. In this context, they use the Internet to provide a place to publish student work; access information and conduct research; communicate and share ideas; and collaborate.

Even the teachers at Hillside have their own home pages. Sharry Lammers, for example, introduces herself as:

Sharry Lammers

Hi! My name is Sharry Lammers. I am a 6th grade teacher at Hillside Elementary School in Minnesota. The 6th graders in my class have created their own webs. Each student has written a paragraph that best describes themselves. Along with the description, they have added a picture that in one way or another represents them. We look forward to reaching out and communicating with you through the Internet. Please feel free to ask us questions or offer us constructive suggestions.

My e-mail address is LammersS@hillside.sowashco. k12.mn.us

We look forward to hearing from you!

A student in Mrs. Lammers' class, uses a multicolored display of what appear to be fireworks and streamers for her home page. This is her essay, in which she introduces herself:

This is my Home Page

Hi, my name is (student name omitted). I love to figure skate. It's one of my favorite sports. I also like to swim. I'm in level seven. I'm 11 years old, but I'm turning 12 on October 17. I have one sister named Molly, and one brother named Greg. I live in Cottage Grove, Minnesota. I go to Hillside Elementary. I have four pets. Their names are, Herbie (dog), Spice (cat), Areil (goldfish), Flounder (goldfish). I like my cat a lot. He is really funny. One gross thing about him is that he eats bugs. He catches them in mid air and eats them! My goal is to travel around the world, and become a professional figure skater!

Please Write to me!

In addition to student home pages, individual reports and projects are also posted for each class at Cottage Grove. Teachers can even post lesson plans they want to share with others. For example, Dorothy Reid, a third grade teacher at Hillside not only introduces herself on her home page, but also includes her lesson plans for the oceanography project she is conducting with her students. As she explains:

> After 25 years of teaching, making the Internet a part of my profession has rejuvenated me beyond my wildest dreams.
>
> At our family reunion this summer my brother John, who is a teacher at the Monterey Academy of Oceanographic Science (Monterey, California), and I decided to work together on an oceanography unit.
>
> I plan to guide my third graders into their oceanography projects. His high school students will assist us in researching and answering our questions.
>
> I'm looking forward to an exciting year in education for the students and me.
>
> ReidD@hillside.sowashco.k12.mn.us

Oceanography Project

> My initial motivating force to begin the Oceanography Project was a discussion with my brother John, who is currently teaching at the Monterey Academy of Oceanographic Sciences. We decided our main theme would be oceanography but we saw as equally important the use of technology to accomplish our goals of the third graders obtaining a better understanding of the ocean and its effects on their lives and his high school students researching some of our ocean questions.
>
> I sent an information letter to the parents explaining the project and requesting their permission for their child to participate.
>
> My main source of information for the theme came from the book Project Aquatic.

Under the general heading of oceanography, the students had to choose a particular area of interest. Finally the students were given the expectations for their projects.

District Outcomes

♦ Communication

Applies effective strategies to comprehend print:

1. Selects reading materials based on goals and purposes
2. Poses questions to be answered by reading and researching
3. Activates knowledge of subject prior to reading
4. Relates new information to prior knowledge
5. Retells and summarizes material
6. Reads fluently
7. Uses corrective strategies when text is not comprehended

Applies effective strategies in written communication:

1. Writes in a variety of genres
2. Writes considering the purpose and audience
3. Synthesizes and organizes information
4. Uses process writing
5. Demonstrates growth in use of spelling, grammar, and mechanicics.

Communicates effectively using oral language:

1. Communicates ideas in a logical order
2. Speaks clearly and audibly
3. Shares experiences and information

Demonstrates active listening behavior

♦ Math

Explain reasonableness of answers in length
Use multiple strategies to solve problems
Develop the process of measuring using standard and nonstandard units of measurement.

Collect, organize and interpret data to solve problems

♦ Science

Recognize a subsystem as a system that is part of another system
Describe some of the variables of system earth
Examine the effect of birth and death on the size of a population of organisms
Explain the factors limiting the numbers of plants and animals surviving in each generation
Illustrate the concepts of food chains and food webs
Describe the feeding interactions among aquatic populations

Minnesota State Graduation Standards

Element One: Grade Three: 31.G3.1
Element One: Grade Three: 31.G3.2
Element Two: Grade Three: 32.G3.1 Procedural 3-4.
Element Four: Grade Three 34.G3.2
Element Five: Grade Three 35.G3.1
Element Six: Grade Three 36.G3.1

Lessons

Lesson One
Lesson Two
Lesson Three
Lesson Four
Lesson Five
Lesson Six
Lesson Seven
Lesson Eight
Lesson Nine
Lesson Ten
Lesson Eleven
Lesson Twelve
Lesson Thirteen
Lesson Fourteen
Lesson Fifteen

Mrs. Reid's lesson plans have numerous hyperlinks, which, unfortunately, cannot be shown in these examples. She has demonstrated how teachers can use the Internet to not only further develop their own ideas about curriculum, but also to share them with others. Visiting the Hillside Web site should provide you with an excellent idea of how the Internet can be integrated across an entire school's curriculum.

Hillside Elementary School, Cottage Grove, Minnesota
http://hillside.coled.umn.edu/

Student home pages can become quite sophisticated. You can see this by visiting the Bronx High School of Science. One student's home page, for example, begins with a cool cartoon and his personal biography.

My Personal Biography

Hi! My name is (student name omitted). Anyway, I am currently a senior at The Bronx High School of Science. I was born in Seoul, Korea, on May 14, 1979. I now live in Flushing Queens of NYC. My hobbies are Basketball, Swimming, Volleyball, Video Games, and Computers. Some of the classes I am taking are Advanced C Programming, GMO, and Internet-working Projects. Well, thats it! Whew nice and short. Hope I didn't bore you! Anyway, enjoy what I have on my Homepage.

This student's home page includes a link to information about his school, Web pages he has created, Internet Resources, WWW Search Engines, places of interest such as Moscow Channel, Scientific American, Dark Alliance, PlanetOut, JNCO Jeans Co., as well as links to Korean Music that he is interested in, movies he plans to see, and links to his friends on the Internet.

The Bronx High School of Science
http://www.bxscience.edu/

When looking at school Web sites from across the country, and around the world, you can find an incredible number of good ideas for activities and projects with students. At St. Mark's School in Boise, Idaho, students in the fifth grade are studying different regions of the United States and are requesting people visiting their Web site to send them photographs of where they live. As they explain:

> We would like to have people from other places send us photographs which represent their part of the country. Please include what the photo is and a little information about it. Either e-mail it or send it by regular mail and we will scan it and put it on our home page. Be sure to check back to see pictures from across this great country of ours.

St. Mark's Catholic School, Boise, Idaho
http://www.cyberhighway.net/~stmarks/

The request for photographs from around the world by students at St. Mark's is a relatively simple project. A more sophisticated project in much the same spirit illustrates CU-SeeMe technology being used at Ligon Gifted and Talented Middle School in Raleigh, North Carolina.

CU-SeeMe technology is essentially a videophone system for the Internet that allows users to see each other between distant sites. The technology is extremely affordable (a black and white camera is less than $100) and presents great opportunities for schools with their own web sites to connect up to one another.

Caroline McCullen, a teacher at Ligon describes how her students are using CU-SeeMe technology:

How are We Using CU-SeeMe?

We use CU-SeeMe in a variety of ways. We meet with students and teachers who contribute to Mid-Link Magazine to plan our articles and projects. When a teacher needs information from a professional or subject area expert, we try to find someone who can answer those questions. Last year we joined Craig Nelson, captain of the NOAA MALCOLM BALDRIGE, to discuss his findings regarding water quality and global warming. You can see the details of this exciting virtual meeting at our Web site.

This year we plan to meet students in Belarus, Africa, Florida, and a variety of other locations. Most of our conferences are related to the academic content in our middle school curriculum. We are always interested in helping schools practice their CU-SeeMe sessions for their appointed "big event." If you want to practice, please send us e-mail. We need to practice, too!

Ligon Gifted and Talented Magnet Middle School, Raleigh, North Carolina
   http://www2.ncsu.edu/ncsu/cep/ligon/ligon. home.html

Many schools are making good use of the Internet for non-academic purposes. Mountain View Elementary School in Layton, Utah, for example, includes information about the school, its teachers and its student council, as well as the lunch menu!

Mountain View Elementary School
   http://www.apeleon.net/~mtview

11

JUST FOR FUN

The Internet and the World Wide Web are places for doing serious work, but they are also places whose sites can be explored just for the fun of it. Here are some web sites students will enjoy visiting just for the fun of it.

All sorts of information about the Oscars and current films.

Academy of Motion Picture Arts & Science
   http:/www.grainger.uiuc.edu/ugl/media/
   oscarind.htm

An electronic version of the complete text of *Alice's Adventures in Wonderland.*

Alice's Adventures in Wonderland
   http://www.cs.cmu.edu/People/rgs/
   alice-ftitle.html

This is a gateway to exhibits of online artists from around the world.

The (Art)^n Laboratory
   http://www.artn.nwu.edu/index.html

Original illustrations such as this one of the March Hare from *Alice in Wonderland* can be found at many Web sites

An interactive coloring book for students K-3 level.

Carlos' Interactive Coloring Book
http://www.ravenna.com/coloring/

Everything you wanted to know about carousels and merry-go-rounds.

Carousel
http://www.access.digex.net/~rburgess/
carousel_links.html

Very simple color mixing games.

Color Mix Master
http://www.ingenius.com/product/
cyberhd/youth/arcade/colors.htm

A guide to all of your favorite comic strips, as well as information about their creators.

The Comic Strip
  http://www.unitedmedia.com/comics

Create your own newspaper using online resources.

Create Your Own Newspaper
  http://sun.bucknell.edu/~boulter/crayon/

All sorts of information on the National Football League, National Hockey League, and other professional sports.

ESPNET Sportzone
  http://espnet.sportszone.com/

Information on all types of computer games.

The Games Domain
  http://wcl-rs.bham.ac.uk/GamesDomain

A worldwide show-and-tell exhibit where kids can show off their favorite things, their accomplishments, and examples of their artwork.

Global Show-N-Tell
  http://emma.manymedia.com:80/show-n-tell/

Everything you ever wanted to know about the LEGO construction system.

Lego Home Page
  http://www.lego.com/index.html

Corporate sites such as the Lego home page
can provide rich educational resources

Play this game to determine how behavioral choices may affect your lifespan.

The Longevity Game
http://www.northwesternmutual.com/
longevit/longevit.htm

A Web site devoted to art of origami paper-folding.

Origami Page
http://www.cs.ubc.ca/spider/jwu/
origami.html

The Mr. Potato Head Game makes it online.

Edible Starchy Tuber Head
http://winnie.acsu.buffalo.edu/potatoe/
potatoe.html

This is the site to go to for everything about the world of roller coasters, who ride them, where they are located and which are the scariest.

Roller Coasters
http://sunsite.unc.edu/darlene/coaster/FAQ/
faq.cover.html

12

CONCLUSION

The invention of the printed book in the late fifteenth century changed the nature of knowledge and learning in Western culture. Printed books provided the technical reference sources for the development of modern science, geography, and a host of other subjects. Art forms such as the novel were invented as a result of modern printing. Schools and universities as we know them today were made possible by the invention of books.

Whether the Internet and the World Wide Web are as profound a revolution in the distribution of knowledge and learning as the printing press was is not clear. It is clear, however, that they are enormously important.

The microcomputer revolution of the late 1970s made it possible for computers to be integrated into our schools on a widespread basis. The introduction of the Internet and the World Wide Web, beginning in the early to mid-1990s represents the introduction of networked knowledge on a global basis in the schools and in the curriculum.

This extraordinary resource is in its infancy. It has yet to fully realize its potential contribution to developing and extending the curriculum. It seems clear that the Internet and the World Wide Web will continue to evolve—and in the end probably take on forms that we can only begin to imagine.

The challenge for educators is ultimately a curricular rather than a technical one. How can this extraordinary resource best be used to educate students and to help teachers achieve their goals of instruction?

As the manuscript for this book was being completed, the Mars Pathfinder Lander was transmitting its first images of the surface of Mars back to Earth. The images from the landing were put onto Web sites almost as soon as they were received. I believe that the images from Pathfinder are a fitting representation of the types of extraordinary resources that are increasingly available to schools on the Internet and the World Wide Web and that are changing the character of the classroom and what we can teach.

I hope that examples such as this, together with this book, help you take on the curricular challenge posed by the Internet and the World Wide Web. There are few better opportunities to improve our schools and the education of our children.

The surface of Mars showing the Pathfinder mission's rover "Sojourner" and "Twin Peaks."

Links to the Mars Pathfinder Web Pages
    http://www.jpl.nasa.gov/mpfmir/
National Space Science Data Center Mars Photo Gallery
    http://nssdc.gsfc.nasa.gov/photo_gallery/
    photogallery-mars.html
Mars Today Poster of Current Conditions on Mars
    http://humbabe.arc.nasa.gov/

APPENDIX A

BIBLIOGRAPHY

This bibliography includes both works referred to in this book and materials that are of particular usefulness to those interested in going into certain selected topics in more detail. Particularly noteworthy articles and books are annotated.

Armstrong, Sara, *A Pocket Tour of the Kidstuff on the Internet* (San Francisco: Sybex, 1996).

This is a brief and extremely useful introduction to the Internet for children. In Part 1, readers are given instructions for using the basic tools of the Internet. Part 2 provides a list of excellent Internet sites for children.

Bailey, Elaine K., and Morton Cotlar, "Teaching Via the Internet," *Communication Education*, April 1994, Vol. 43, No. 2, p. 159.

Borland, Candace M., "Arts EdNet: Arts Education Resources on the Internet," *School Arts*, January 1996, Vol. 95, p. 12.

Bowers, C. A. , *The Cultural Dimensions of Educational Computing: Understanding the Non-Neutrality of Technology* (New York: Teachers College Press, 1980).

A seminal work in the field of educational computing. Bowers brilliantly argues the limitations inherent in many contemporary computer applications and uses in the schools.

Bruning, David, "Students in Cyberspace," *Astronomy*, October 1995, Vol. 23, No. 10, p. 48.

Cerf, Vinton G., "Networks," *Scientific American*, Vol. 265, No. 3, September 1991, pp. 72–81.

A useful introduction to computer networks.

Cuban, Larry, *Teachers and Machines: The Classroom Use of Technology Since 1920* (New York: Teachers College Press, 1986).

This is perhaps the most thoughtful work available on how teachers have historically used technology in their classrooms. It includes discussions about computers and earlier innovations such as film, radio, and educational television. Cuban's major contribution lies in his recognition that technology often is not embraced by teachers as a result of its failure to meet the actual circumstances under which they do their work.

Cummins, Jim, and Dennis Sayers, *Brave New Schools: Challenging Cultural Illiteracy through Global Learning Networks* (New York: St. Martin's Press, 1995).

An extremely interesting exploration of the potential of the Internet to open new models of cultural literacy and awareness in the schools. Besides providing an insightful theoretical discussion, this book is made even more useful by its excellent guide to Internet resources for parents and teachers.

Dertouzos, Micahel L., "Communications, Computers and Networks," *Scientific American*, September 1991, pp. 62–69.

An extremely interesting introduction to computers and computer networks by the director of the Laboratory for Computer Science at M.I.T. for a special issue on Communications, Computers and Networks," for the *Scientific American*.

Dyrli, Odvard Egil, "Surfing the World Wide Web to Education Hot-spots," *Technology & Learning*, October 1995, Vol. 16, No. 2, p. 44.

Dyrli, Odvard Egil, and Daniel E. Kinnaman, "Connecting Classrooms: School is More than a Place," *Technology & Learning*, May-June 1995, Vol. 15, No. 8, p. 82.

Dyrli, Odvard Egil, and Daniel E. Kinnaman, "Teaching Effectively with Telecommunications," *Technology & Learning*, February 1996, Vol. 16, No. 5, p. 56.

Evan, Tessa Perry, "Blackout: Preventing Racial Discrimination on the Net," *Library Journal*, September 15, 1995, Vol. 120, No. 15, p. 44.

Frazier, Gloria G., and Deneen Frazier, *Telecommunications and Education: Surfing and the Art of Change* (Alexandria, VA: National School Boards Association, 1994).

An extremely useful introduction to telecommunications and the schools. This report provides background, planning tools, and resource information that is invaluable to anyone interested in starting to use online services in the schools.

Gibson, William, *Neuromancer* (New York: Ace, 1984).

The novel that introduces the term cyberspace. Gibson's novels are among the best recent works in science fiction and anticipate many likely developments in computing and culture. Also see his books *Count Zero, Mona Lisa Overdrive,* and, with Bruce Sterling, *The Difference Engine.*

Harris, Judi, *Way of the Ferret—Finding and Using Educational Resources on the Internet* (Eugene, OR: International Society for Technology in Education, 1996).

Kaplan, R. D., "The Coming Anarchy," *Atlantic Monthly,* February 1994, pp. 44–76.

Kinnaman, Daniel E., "Leapfrog is not an Olympic Sport (The Benefits of Installing a School LAN Before Connecting to the World Wide Web)," *Technology & Learning,* September 1995, Vol. 16, No. 1, p. 90.

Kelly, M. G., "Mining Mathematics on the Internet," *Arithmetic Teacher,* January 1994, Vol. 41, No. 5, p. 276.

Kroll, Ed, *The Whole Internet User's Guide & Catalog* (Sebastapol, CA: O'Reilly & Associates, Inc., 1992).

An excellent introduction and handbook on all major aspects of the Internet.

McLuhan, Marshall, *Understanding Media: The Extensions of Man* (New York: Mentor Books, 1964). MIT Press reprinted *Understanding Media* in a 30th anniversary edition in 1994 with a new introduction by Lewis Lapham.

McLuhan is frequently disregarded as a pop scholar of the 1960s. His ideas about media have profound implications for contemporary culture and are well worth revisiting.

Meagher, Mary Elaine, "Learning English on the Internet," *Educational Leadership,* October 1995, Vol. 23, No. 10, p. 48.

MacFarquhar, Neil, "The Internet Goes to School, and Educators Debate," *The New York Times*, March 7, 1996, Vol. 145, pp. C2 and B1.

Moore, Dinty W. , *The Emperor's Virtual Clothes: The Naked Truth about Internet Culture* (Chapel Hill, NC: Algonquin Books, 1995).

Moursond, David, *Obtaining Resources for Technology in Education—A How-To Guide for Writing Proposals, Forming Partnerships, and Raising Funds* (Eugene, OR: International Society for Technology in Education, 1996).

A detailed sourcebook on how to obtain funding for hardware, software, staff development, curriculum materials, and consulting services for educational computing.

Nader, R., "Citizens and Computers," *Utne Reader*, No. 68, March-April 1995, p. 74.

Negroponte, Nicholas, *Being Digital* (New York: Alfred Knopf, 1995).

One of the gurus of contemporary computing and multimedia reflects on how our lives are being transformed as a result of "being digital."

Norris, Alison, "A Passport to the World Community," *Times Educational Supplement*, November 10, 1995, No. 4141, p. 38.

O'Connell, Kenneth, "E-mail and Art Education," *School Arts*, May 1994, Vol. 93, No. 9, p. 10.

Office of Technology Assessment, Congress of the United States, *Teachers & Technology: Making the Connection*, OTA-EHR-616 (Washington: U. S. Government Printing Office, April 1995).

This is an extremely valuable assessment of current computer use and technology in American public education. It not only addresses possible uses of current technology, but the needs for teacher training in technology.

Papert, Seymour, *Mindstorms* (New York: Basic Books, 1980).

Papert provides an introduction to his ideas about educational computing and the use of his program LOGO. This is a classic and pioneering work in computers and education.

Papert, Seymour, *The Children's Machine: Rethinking School in the Age of the Computer* (New York: Basic Books, 1992).

Papert outlines an intriguing model of the computer as a machine ideally suited for the child and learning. This book flies in the face of many of the more traditional approaches being used in computer-based instruction and provides a cogent rationale for using the computer as a knowledge tool through which the child can learn how to think and create.

"Public Schools Increase Links to Cyberspace," *The New York Times*, February 18, 1996, Vol. 145, s1 pp. 16 and 32.

Provenzo, Eugene F., Jr., *Beyond the Gutenberg Galaxy: Microcomputers and the Emergence of Post-Typographic Culture* (New York: Teachers College Press, 1986).

Although somewhat dated, this book by the author, argues that the introduction of the micro- or personal computer represents a technological and deeply cultural revolution similar to the type of change that occurred as a result of the Gutenberg revolution.

Provenzo, Eugene F., Jr., *Video Kids: Making Sense of Nintendo* (Cambridge: Harvard University Press, 1991).

A comprehensive analysis of video games—particularly those produced by the Nintendo Corporation—and the ways in which children learn and construct reality through them.

Provenzo, Eugene F., Jr., "The Video Generation," *The American School Board Journal*, Vol. 179, number 3, pp. 29–32.

This article provides a general summary of the main ideas in Provenzo's book *Video Kids*.

Rheingold, Howard, *The Virtual Community: Homesteading on the Electronic Frontier* (Reading, MA: Addison-Wesley Publishing Company, 1993).

A pioneering, if at times naively optimistic, analysis of the Internet as a vehicle for transforming culture and communication.

Rose, Allen D., "Financing Technology," *The American School Board Journal*, July 1992, Vol. 178, No. 7, pp. 17–19.

Sayers, D., and K. Brown, "Bilingual Education and Telecommunications: A Perfect Fit," *The Computing Teacher*, 1987, Vol. 17, pp. 23–24.

Sullivan, E. V., "Computers, Culture, and Educational Futures: A Critical Appraisal," *Interchange*, Vol. 14, No. 3, pp. 17–26.

Solomon, Gwen, "Where and How to Get Grants," *Electronic Learning*, January 1991, Vol. 10, No. 4, pp. 16–19.

Solomon, Gwen, "All About Grants," *Electronic Learning*, February 1993, Vol. 12, No. 5, pp. 14–23.

An excellent introductory guide to grantsmanship and educational computing.

"Surfing Made Easy," *NEA Today*, Decemeber 1995, Vol. 14, No. 5, p. 25.

Turkle, Sherry, *Life on the Screen: Identity in the Age of the Internet* (New York: Simon & Schuster, 1995).

Turkle, author of *The Second Self: Computers and the Human Spirit* and a professor at the Massachusetts Institute of Technology, provides a compelling examination of how our ideas about how our psychological selves, as well as our ideas about machines and what it is to be human, are being redefined in the era of the Internet.

Turlington, Shannon, *Walking the World Wide Web: Your Personal Guide to the Best of the Web* (Chapel Hill, NC: Ventana Press, 1995).

This is an excellent introduction to the World Wide Web. For those readers interested in becoming much more involved in exploring the Web, this type of source is essential reading. Software accompanies the book.

Wilde, Candee, "The Internet & Electronic Commerce: A Revolution Begins," *The New York Times*, March 24, 1996, Special Advertising Section, p. 21F.

Wujcik, Anne, Geral Bailey, Dan Lumley, and Anne Ward, editors, *Plans & Policies for Technology in Education: A Compendium* (Alexandria, VA: National School Boards Association, 1994).

A compendium of technology plans from school districts across the country assembled by the National School Boards Association. A very helpful document for those wanting technology plans, as well as models for job descriptions in technology and survey forms.

APPENDIX B

ACCEPTABLE USE POLICIES AND FORMS

School districts across the country are establishing Acceptable Use Policies and protocols for using the Internet. The Bellingham School District in Bellingham, Washington has created a particularly good set of Acceptable Use guidelines. They are included here with the permission of the school district and may be used for nonprofit purposes.

Bellingham School District
    http://www.bham.wednet.edu

Bellingham School District 501
2313P
Administrative Procedures
Student Access to Networked Information
Resources Procedures

1. PROGRAM DEVELOPMENT

In order to match electronic resources as closely as possible to the approved district curriculum, district personnel will review and evaluate resources in order to offer "home pages" and menus of materials which comply with Board guidelines listed in Board Policy 2311 governing the selection of instructional materials. In this manner, staff will provide developmentally appropriate guidance to students as they make use of telecommunications and electronic information resources to conduct research and other studies related to the district curriculum. All students will be informed by staff of their rights and responsibilities as users of the district network prior to gaining access to that network, either as an individual user or as a member of a class or group.

As much as possible, access to district information resources will be designed in ways which point students to those which have been reviewed and evaluated prior to use. While students may be able to move beyond those resources to others which have not been evaluated by staff, they shall be provided with guidelines and lists of resources particularly suited to the learning objectives. Students may pursue electronic research independent of staff supervision only if they have been granted parental permission and have submitted all required forms. Permission is not transferable and may not be shared.

1. INTERNET RULES

Students are responsible for good behavior on school computer networks just as they are in a classroom or a school hallway. Communications on the network are often public in nature. General school rules for behavior and communications apply.

The network is provided for students to conduct research and communicate with others. Independent access to network services is provided to students who agree to act in a considerate and responsible manner. Parent permission is required for minors. Access is a privilege, not a right. Access entails responsibility.

Individual users of the district computer networks are responsible for their behavior and communications over those networks. It is presumed that users will comply with district standards and will honor the agreements they have signed.

Network storage areas may be treated like school lockers. Network administrators may review files and communications to maintain system integrity and insure that users are using the system responsibly. Users should not expect that files stored on district servers will always be private.

During school, teachers of younger students will guide them toward appropriate materials. Outside of school, families bear responsibility for such guidance as they must also exercise with information sources such as television, telephones, movies, radio, and other potentially offensive media.

The following are not permitted:

Sending or displaying offensive messages or pictures
Using obscene language
Harassing, insulting or attacking others
Damaging computers, computer systems or computer networks
Violating copyright laws
Using others' passwords
Trespassing in others' folders, work or files
Intentionally wasting limited resources
Employing the network for commercial purposes

1. SANCTIONS

1. Violations may result in a loss of access.

2. Additional disciplinary action may be determined at the building level in line with existing practice regarding inappropriate language or behavior.

3. When applicable, law enforcement agencies may be involved.

Approved: April 27, 1995
Dale E. Kinsley
Superintendent of Schools

Bellingham Public Schools

Parent Permission Letter
Internet and Electronic Mail Permission Form

The Bellingham Public Schools

We are pleased to offer students of the Bellingham Public Schools access to the district computer network for electronic mail and the Internet. To gain access to e-mail and the Internet, all students under the age of 18 must obtain parental permission and must sign and return this form to the LIBRARY MEDIA SPECIALIST. Students 18 and over may sign their own forms.

Access to e-mail and the Internet will enable students to explore thousands of libraries, databases, and bulletin boards while exchanging messages with Internet users throughout the world. Families should be warned that some material accessible via the Internet may contain items that are illegal, defamatory, inaccurate or potentially offensive to some people. While our intent is to make Internet access available to further educational goals and objectives, students may find ways to access other materials as well. We believe that the benefits to students from access to the Internet, in the form of information resources and opportunities for collaboration, exceed any disadvantages. But ultimately, parents and guardians of minors are responsible for setting and conveying the standards that their children should follow when using media and information sources. To that end, the Bellingham Public Schools support and respect each family's right to decide whether or not to apply for access.

District Internet and E-Mail Rules

Students are responsible for good behavior on school computer networks just as they are in a classroom or a school hallway. Communications on the network are often public in nature. General school rules for behavior and communications apply.

The network is provided for students to conduct research and communicate with others. Access to network services is given to students who agree to act in a considerate and responsible manner. Parent permission is required. Access is a privilege—not a right. Access entails responsibility.

Individual users of the district computer networks are responsible for their behavior and communications over those networks. It is presumed that users will comply with district standards and will honor the agreements they have signed. Beyond the clarification of such standards, the district is not responsible for restricting, monitoring or controlling the communications of individuals utilizing the network.

Network storage areas may be treated like school lockers. Network administrators may review files and communications to maintain system integrity and insure that users are using the system responsibly. Users should not expect that files stored on district servers will always be private.

Within reason, freedom of speech and access to information will be honored. During school, teachers of younger students will guide them toward appropriate materials. Outside of school, families bear the same responsibility for such guidance as they exercise with information sources such as television, telephones, movies, radio, and other potentially offensive media.

As outlined in Board policy and procedures on student rights and responsibilities (3200), copies of which are available in school offices, the following are not permitted:

Sending or displaying offensive messages or pictures

Using obscene language

Harassing, insulting or attacking others

Damaging computers, computer systems or computer networks

Violating copyright laws

Using another's password

Trespassing in another's folders, work or files

Intentionally wasting limited resources

Employing the network for commercial purposes

Violations may result in a loss of access as well as other disciplinary or legal action.

User Agreement and Parent Permission Form—1995

As a user of the Bellingham Public Schools computer network, I hereby agree to comply with the above stated rules—communicating over the network in a reliable fashion while honoring all relevant laws and restrictions.

Student Signature _____

As the parent or legal guardian of the minor student signing above, I grant permission for my son or daughter to access networked computer services such as electronic mail and the Internet. I understand that individuals and families may be held liable for violations. I understand that some materials on the Internet may be objectionable, but I accept responsibility for guidance of Internet use—setting and conveying standards for my daughter or son to follow when selecting, sharing or exploring information and media.

Parent Signature _____Date _____

Name of Student _____

School _____Grade _____

Soc. Sec.#_____ Birth Date _____

Street Address _____ Home Telephone _____

Bellingham School District 501
5260
Board Policy
Staff Access to Networked Information Resources

With the spread of telecommunications throughout the modern work place, the Board recognizes that employees will shift the ways they share ideas, transmit information, and contact others. As staff members are connected to the global community, their use of new tools and systems brings new responsibilities as well as opportunities.

The Board expects that all employees will learn to use electronic mail and telecommunications tools and apply them daily in appropriate ways to the performance of tasks associated with their positions and assignments. Toward that end, the Board directs the Superintendent to provide staff with training in the proper and effective use of telecommunications and electronic mail.

Communication over networks should not be considered private. Network supervision and maintenance may require review and inspection of directories or messages. Messages may sometimes be diverted accidentally to a destination other than the one intended. Privacy in these communications is not guaranteed. The district reserves the right to access stored records in cases where there is reasonable cause to expect wrong-doing or misuse of the system. Courts have ruled that old messages may be subpoenaed, and network supervisors may examine communications in order to ascertain compliance with network guidelines for acceptable use.

The Board directs the Superintendent to specify those behaviors which are permitted and those which are not permitted, as well as appropriate procedures to guide employee use. In general, employees are expected to communicate in a professional manner consistent with state laws governing the behavior of school employees and with federal laws governing copyrights. Electronic mail and telecommunications are not to be utilized to share confidential information about students or other employees.

The Board encourages staff to make use of telecommunications to explore educational topics, conduct research, and contact others in the educational world. The Board anticipates that the new systems will expedite the sharing of effective practices and lessons across the district and will help staff stay on the leading edge of practice by forming partnerships with others across the nation and around the world.

Adopted: January 25, 1996

Parent Permission Form for World Wide Web Publishing of Student Work

Name of Student _____

School _____ Name of Parent _____

We understand that our daughter or son's artwork or writing is under consideration for publication on the World Wide Web, a part of the Internet. We further understand that the work will appear with a copyright notice prohibiting the copying of such work without express written permission. In the event anyone requests such permission, those requests will be forwarded to us as parents. No home address or telephone number will appear with such work.

We grant permission for the World Wide Web publishing as described above until June of 1998. A copy of all such publishing will be printed out and brought home for us to see.

Name_____

Date _____

Name_____

Date _____

I, the student, also give my permission for such publishing.

Name_____

Date _____

Permission is granted to copy and use this form.

APPENDIX C

"WHAT IS?" INDEX

Throughout this book there are boxed definitions. These are intended to provide an introduction to terms and concepts you may frequently hear spoken about and used in conjunction with the Internet and the World Wide Web, but with which you may not be familiar. The following alphabetical index is intended as a quick guide to help you make ready reference to these terms.